W9-BYY-401

LET·MY
PEOPLE
GO

LET·MY PEOPLE GO

EMPOWERING LAITY·FOR·MINISTRY

ALVIN J. LINDGREN AND
NORMAN SHAWCHUCK

Abingdon

Nashville

LET MY PEOPLE GO

Copyright © 1980 by Abingdon

Second Printing 1981

All rights reserved.
No part of this book may be reproduced in any manner
whatsoever without written permission of the publisher
except brief quotations embodied in critical articles
or reviews. For information address Abingdon,
Nashville, Tennessee

Library of Congress Cataloging in Publication Data

LINDGREN, ALVIN J
  Let my people go.
  Bibliography: p.
  Includes index.
  1. Christian leadership.   I. Shawchuck, Norman, 1935-   joint
author.   II. Title.
  BV652.1.L56   253   80-16035

ISBN 0-687-21377-0

Scripture quotations noted RSV are from the Revised Standard Version
Common Bible, copyrighted © 1973, by the Division of Christian
Education of the National Council of the Churches of Christ in the U.S.A.,
and used by permission.

Scripture quotations noted NEB are from the New English Bible © the
Delegates of the Oxford University Press and the Syndics of the
Cambridge University Press 1961, 1970. Reprinted by permission.

The scripture quotation noted NASB is from the New American Standard
Bible, © the Lockman Foundation 1960, 1962, 1963, 1968, 1971, 1972,
1973, 1975.

MANUFACTURED BY THE PARTHENON PRESS AT
NASHVILLE, TENNESSEE, UNITED STATES OF AMERICA

CONTENTS

LET·MY
PEOPLE
GO

PREFACE

The basic concept underlying this book began a long time ago. From the time of Moses, one of the distinctive threads found woven throughout the biblical story is a recurring emphasis on setting free the people of God to serve him.

God called Moses to free his people from Egyptian slavery. Before each plague, Moses stood before Pharaoh as God's spokesman and said, "Let my people go, that they may serve me" (Exod. 8:1 RSV) That call was not simply for political freedom, but for freedom so that they might serve God. The freeing of people to serve God is a recurring theme of Scripture and history. The Old Testament recounts continuing struggles to free God's people from being entrapped by idols, secular culture, nationalism, selfishness, and even priestly legalism. The good news of the New Testament is that Christ came to free us from sin and death. Christ clashed head on with the priestly legalism of his day from which he sought to free people to serve God.

The New Testament views the church as "the people of God" and "Christ's Body." the concept of the priesthood of all believers clearly calls all Christians to God's service.

Somehow, over the years, the clergy became the dominant force in the decisions and life of the church. The authors believe that in our day, God's spirit is again saying to the church and its' leaders, "Let my people go, that they might serve me."

This book is written for those who believe that the increased involvement and empowerment of lay persons in the church is sorely needed today.

The writers firmly believe that the future of the Christian church will be shaped by how clergy and lay members regard one another and collaborate in the church's ministry. The clergy cannot do the work of the church, nor can they be the church. Neither can the work of the church be done by the clergy utilizing a handful of faithful lay persons as extensions of their ministry. Likewise, in our sophisticated, technical society, laity alone cannot do their full-time secular jobs and do the work of the church on a part-time basis without the trained leadership of the clergy. The church's reason for being is to make known the meaning of God's love and increase its expression in the life of persons and in the corporate lie of society. For this mission God calls both clergy and laity to collaborate as co-workers.

A major concern of both clergy and laity must be the discovery of how laity can be enlisted and equipped to increase the church's ability to enact the gospel in all areas of personal and contemporary society's complex concerns. Today's needs and concerns are such that only team work of lay persons and clergy can affect social structure and personal life-styles. If the church is to make a corporate witness and impact today, increased lay involvement in every area of the church's life is essential.

This book will lift up key areas in church life that can challenge and equip lay members to assume much larger and more significant roles in every aspect of the life of the church. Clergy have a crucial responsibility to create the climate and to provide opportunity, challenge, and the necessary training that will enable lay persons to effectively assume a large role in the church. Likewise, laity have a responsibility to facilitate their own involvement through utilizing the many skills they possess, and by using their relationships with other persons to enact the gospel through the church's work and ministry. They have knowledge and contacts to enlarge the ministry of the clergy.

Underlying the response of clergy and lay persons alike to the church's ministry must be a deepening spiritual pilgrimage toward understanding the gospel and a commitment to its enactment in society.

Chapter 1

Spiritual Formation

I. Introduction

The empowerment of laity and clergy to become active co-workers as God's people is the key to a vital church tomorrow. If God's mission is to be furthered through the church's ministry, then a way must be found to engage more of God's people in ministering to one another and to the world's needs. That is precisely what this book is about.

In an ecumenical conference for laity in 1978, Judge Genevieve Blatt of Pennsylvania, speaking as a lay person said: "For too long we have been looking to clergy to do everything that needs to be done. I feel now there is something for us to do."[1] It is indeed true that for centuries the church has been dominated by the clergy. They established the creeds and theological positions, developed church structure, laid down church laws, and established liturgical and worship patterns. On the other hand, it is also true that in recent church conferences there is a significant trend emerging focusing on the laity as a commanding new force in the church. The domination of the church by the clergy is declining. More and more it is being recognized that an overworked clergy and an underused laity constitute a self-perpetuating kind of entrapment.

The movement toward seeking greater layinvolvement in the church cuts across denominational and theological lines. It can be seen in such differing groups as the charismatic movement, social-action groups in many denominations, and the evangelical movement, as well as in the search by many for new forms of "lay" theology (e.g. liberation, women, blacks) The thrust toward greater lay involvement is significant in the Roman Catholic Church as well as in most Protestant denominations. Let us be perfectly clear: A high degree of lay involvement in the church has not yet arrived; but there is a growing recognition that it is needed, and it is on the way in varying degrees in different settings. It is also clear that an increasing mutual ministry of clergy and laity faces many difficulties in its emergence in the life of the church. It is our intention to chart courses of action that will facilitate movement toward the goal of increased lay involvement in the church's ministry.

What underlies the current thrust toward greater lay involvement in the church and increased "democratization" of church life? It may be helpful to mention a few of the major forces such as: increasing education and economic power of laity; the trend toward democratization of society in political, economic, and educational arenas, as well as on the religious front, as evidenced in the Second Vatican Council; and increased lay membership and voting in Protestant denominational bodies. One interesting dynamic initiating a move toward greater lay involvement in church affairs is the conservative lay reaction against the involvement of many clergy in the social activism of the 1960s.

It needs to be also pointed out that there is a more positive dynamic at work toward lay involvement in the church. Increasing numbers of lay persons have become spiritually alive and sensitive to the needs of persons and issues facing society today. These persons are on a serious spiritual pilgrimage. They have also become committed to the church as a viable institution in today's world to meet those needs. It is toward the enlargement of this group of laity that this book is focused.

Unfortunately, it cannot be assumed that all clergy are

ready for or will welcome laity as genuine co-workers in a mutual ministry in the life and work of the church. As the power of the laity increases, the power of the clergy decreases. Some clergy have a strong need to be the dominant controlling factor in the church. Such pastors want only carefully controlled lay involvement through their giving of assignments to the laity, rather than involving them in planning and decision making about the church's ministry regarding what should be done and who should do it. Such clergy need help in letting go, and some want such help—both in understanding themselves, and in developing ways in which they can change to accept and enable laity to join them in the church's ministry. It is precisely this kind of help we hope to give in this volume.

II. God's Mission—Our Ministry

The undergirding theological assumption of this book is that the mission is God's—the ministry is ours as God's people. This is how we understand the church. We are called into existence to minister in God's name so that his mission can come about. What an overwhelming call and challenge!

God created us to be in relationship and fellowship with himself. We are created in God's own image. God so respected us that we are given the power of choice, even choosing to separate ourselves from God. God's mission from the beginning was and is to bring us into relationship with himself and through that to relate to one another. "God so loved the world that he gave . . . " (John 3:16) is one way of pinpointing God's mission. Jesus made it quite clear that he came that "we might see the Father" through him. God's mission is to bind all persons to himself so that through that relationship we are bound to one another.

God's mission is to come about through persons by whose ministry God seeks us to accept his love and fellowship. God's treasure (mission) is in earthen vessels. This has been so since creation. God seeks to

15

reach us in many ways, but persons have been the primary means through which God has expressed himself. Throughout the Old Testament, God used persons to communicate himself to the human race. Call the roll: Abraham, Moses, David, Amos, Isaiah, and Jeremiah, to name a few. In Jesus, God became incarnate in human form to enable all to understand his mission, and through Jesus' death on the cross make it possible for every human being to know and accept his love. The New Testament records the ministry of the disciples, Paul and others, giving themselves as instruments through whom God's mission of love for all, through Christ, might be realized. Indeed, the mission *is* God's and the ministry is ours. God calls the church to the ministry of his mission. God's treasure (mission) is indeed in us, earthen and inadequate vessels though we are.

The high calling of the church is to minister in God's name. This calling is to laity and clergy alike, to all of God's people. Indeed, God did not first create clergy and then laity. All are called to be God's ambassadors to minister in his name.

The awesomeness of being called to be God's representative and minister came home to me one summer in a most unusual and unexpected way. I was fishing on a lake with my junior-high-school son. Since the fish were not biting, we were talking about all kinds of things. Out of the blue I was asked, "Dad, what is the toughest thing God ever tried to do?" This question caught me off guard, so I responded: "Son, you must have thought about this question some since you are asking it. What do you think?" He responded, "Even though you are a minister you don't know too much about God do you?" He then went on to answer his own question. "Since taking science in school I thought the creation of the world might be the hardest thing God ever tried to do. In Sunday school we got to talking about some of the miracles, like Jesus' resurrection, and I thought that might be the toughest thing God ever did." Before I could respond he went on. "After thinking some more and talking to some people, I have decided no one really knows God very well, so now I think the toughest thing God ever tried to do is to get us to understand who he is and that he loves us." My response simply was,"I think you are right." I was overwhelmed at the wisdom of a boy and what his insight implied for me as a minister of a church. I believe he is right. God's mission is "tough," in the words of a junior -high boy. I also believe he has put God's mission very succinctly—" to get us to understand who he is and that he loves us."

If that is God's mission, then Christian laity and clergy alike, as God's people, are called to a ministry of bringing this mission about with God's help. What such a ministry would entail will be explored further throughout these pages.

A. Theological Concepts of Church
That Take Lay Members Seriously

One conclusion of a national lay conference in 1978 with representatives from many denominations, as reported in the *New York Times*, was, "The church has neglected to provide them [laity] with either a solid theological basis for their work, or a sufficiently high status in the church."[2] At this point we would like to focus on some biblical, theological concepts of church that takes lay members seriously. We will deal later with lay status in the church.

The historical rootage of the church is found in the covenant God initiated with Abraham and his children. God called Abraham and said, "Go from your country and your kindred and your father's house to the land that I will show you. And I will make of you a great nation, and I will bless you, and make your name great, so that you will be a blessing" (Gen. 12:1-2 RSV). In responding Israel became God's chosen community. This covenant was renewed in the New Testament with the followers of Christ. "Ye are . . . a royal priesthood, a holy nation, a people of God's own possession, *that you may proclaim the excellencies of Him who has called you . . . "* (I Pet. 2:9 NASB; italics added).

Here is solid grounding for a theology of lay involvement in the ministry of the church. From its beginning the concept of the church as God's chosen community involves four basic ideas:

1. The church is of God (the mission is God's).
2. It was called into being for the purpose of making known God's love (the purpose of the mission).
3. From the outset the church was called and viewed as a corporate community (lifting up the predominant place of the laity).
4. The corporate comunity as a whole, not just priests, has a ministry ("to proclaim the excellencies of him who sent you").

The theological implications of these concepts are myriad and form a solid foundation for developing the corporate ministry of the church as God's people requiring the joint involvement of clergy and laity in its implementation.

Clergy and laity together need to work out the nature of the ministry their local church needs to engage in to effectively communicate the meaning of God's love to their own community and to contemporary society. Theology encompasses more than ideas about God and the history of how he has revealed himself. It also has a current dimension of God's continuing action in our present situation. Clergy and laity need to work out together how they as a community of faith can be the means of ministry for God's mission. In the present tense, theologizing is God at work in the world with his sleeves rolled up. Laity and clergy together need to roll up their sleeves to provide the flesh and blood needed for God to work through them.

This essential corporate nature of the ministry of the church is clearly underscored in the New Testament image of the church as the body of Christ (Ephesians 4 and I Corinthians 12). As Paul spells out in great detail,

18

this understanding of the nature of the church implies many important concepts:

1. The church is Christ's body and he is its head.
2. There is a corporate unity of the church-one body.
3. The church is a continuation of Christ's ministry.
4. The church is to be viewed as a living organism.
5. All members, with very diverse functions, are important and necessary for the body to function.

All these concepts are significantly helpful in developing a theological understanding of the nature of the church. The first four have been treated in detail elsewhere by one of the authors.[3] At this point we should like to lift up the fifth concept for examination because it is particularly relevant for developing a theological basis for the involvement of laity in the ministry of the church.

Paul points out vividly and in great detail that every member of the body is necessary for the body to function. The key to understanding this passage is not the diverse functions of the many parts of the body. The key to the passage is that *the church is compared to the corporate unity of an organic living body*. Only as you view the body as a whole does the marvelous, intricate interrelationship of the parts become evident. When any part of the body does not function properly, the whole body is affected. We do not need to belabor the implications of this analogy in relation to the theological undergirding such a concept gives to the working together of laity and clergy to enable the church to minister in our day as the body of Christ. There is also contained in this concept the framework for dealing with the diversity of gifts and ideas of the many members of a church.

No writer can spell out in specific detail what kinds of programs and actions any church should become involved in because each church body is as different as each human body. However, we believe the biblical framework cited for viewing the church as God's chosen community and the body of Christ provides the context within which laity and clergy must struggle together to work out in detail their own theological basis for ministering in their own situations.

As a matter of fact, the theological concept of the living presence of God through the Holy Spirit requires that the church remain open to God's continuing guidance. God continues too speak to us today. Theologizing is an ongoing activity of the church, or at least it should be. Laity and clergy together must become as sensitive as possible to the message God has for us now and to the meaning of his acts in today's world. Since God has put his treasure in earthen vessels, we are those through whom God's living presence is to be communicated in today's world. This is the calling of clergy and laity alike to ministry today.

B. Biblical Precedent for Lay Involvement in God's Work

Although there is a resurgence of interest in increasing lay involvement in the church's ministry today, it is important to be aware that laity have been called as God's instruments from the beginning. God did not first create clergy and then laity. Clergy (priests), evolved as the nation of Israel became more complex, and some were set aside for special functions. The early leaders of Israel were both political and religious leaders. Joshua, experiencing the overwhelming burden Moses faced as judge of the people, began delegating authority to many other persons; and a structure for involving the "laity" was introduced on a political level. It is clear that God spoke more frequently through lay prophets in the Old Testament than through the designated priests, who frequently were so busy with the details of running the temple and preserving past history that they were insensitive to God's current word that was being revealed. In such a setting the shepherd Amos was called to prophesy. Other prophets rose from the lay ranks to become God's voice to their time.

Even in a male-dominated world, God used Ruth as a messenger in her time. In the New Testament it is interesting that, captive as Paul was to the male superiority complex of the first century, one of the house churches was led by Lydia. She immediately became a "house leader" when converted by Paul, and it was to her house church that Paul and Silas went immediately when getting out of prison (Acts 16:14, 40). It is clear that the New Testament churches Paul's journeys established were dependent for their ongoing survival on the lay persons who led and held them together between Paul's visits and letters. There is no doubt about it; the New Testament church was heavily and even primarily dependent on lay members and leaders.

As a matter of historical fact the church became top-heavy with clerical leadership as the church developed beyond New Testament times. The laity always remained a significant part of the church, but the current move toward greater lay involvement is rooted in the early church.

The bottom line of this statement is that laity should pursue greater involvement in church leadership with a sense of pride, not guilt, and an awareness that the very nature of the church requires their mutual leadership with the clergy. On the other hand, the clergy should not only encourage greater lay involvement in church leadership, but should also equip themselves to enable laity to lead. In fact the New Testament states that various gifts are given different persons "for the enabling of the saints for the work of the ministry (Eph. 4:12).

III. Spiritual Formation and Empowerment

The *beginning point* for a local church that is seeking to engage laity and clergy in ministry to one another and to society is to focus on their mutual spiritual empowerment. What is meant by the term "spiritual empowerment"? This is not easy to answer because it means so many things to different people. Our understanding of spiritual empowerment is that it is an ongoing pilgrimage involving an open search for, and sensitivity to experiencing a growing relationship with God that expresses itself in behavioral action both personally and corporately. A major concern for every church becomes the search for ways to facilitate the spiritual pilgrimage of laity and clergy and to increase their commitment to God's call to minister and witness in his name.

How Do Persons Become Spiritually Empowered?

Spiritual empowerment is a gift of God. Sometimes it comes as a surprise, as were the experiences of Paul on the road to Damascus, and of John Wesley at Aldersgate. In Wesley's case, it came after a long search, but even then the time and place was unexpected. Many have experienced God's presence in their blackest hour of crisis when they thought he had abandoned them. My own awareness of being called into the ordained ministry was a spiritual awakening that came as a "thief in the night." There came a time when I was aware that my life belonged to God and I was to invest my life in the ordained ministry. My *awareness* of this experience came after the fact. I cannot pinpoint any day or hour. It was an experience similar to that of falling in love with my wife. I do not know exactly when I fell in love, but there came a time when I was certain I loved her and wanted to ask her to marry me and to enter a joint commitment to spend our future together. My awareness of God's call for me to commit my life to the ordained ministry was similar. I had been sensitized to God's call and challenge over a period of time and then became aware of what had happened. There is no one pattern of experiencing God's presence in our lives on our spiritual formation pilgrimage.

After a spiritual life retreat at which twelve clergy and twenty-three lay persons were present, I became aware of the extremely varied experiences and situations through which persons perceived that they had become spiritually alive. The group members were invited to share with one another any recent experiences that were significant in their spiritual formation and how these experiences had affected their lives. I was amazed at the variety of situations and experiences shared:

—One person told of experiencing the love of a friend in a time of despondency.

—Another mentioned a pastoral prayer, opening an awareness of God's forgiveness.

—A pastor, while preparing a sermon, heard God's challenge to him as a person.

—The sharing of mutual concerns in a small group brought new life and hope to one member.

—Walking outdoors sparked a sensitivity to God's beauty, dependability, and power that rekindled a flickering flame of faith for one person.

—Participation in a Bible study group had excited one member to become a teacher in the church school to share his newfound understanding with an adult class.

—Working in the Peace Corps had moved one lay person to begin preparation for the ordained ministry.

—A widow, calling in the hospital on one specific occasion, was moved to initiate a continued ministry to the sick three afternoons a week; she now sees herself as God's and her church's representative.

—The support of Christian lay persons and the pastor brought reality to the Christian faith for the first time for one person facing the death of a loved one.

—One man, after he and his wife had lived with her parents for six months, said he had seen authentic practicing Christians for the first time and it "turned my life around."

—Another person had worked on a social action committee that had started a child-care center for working mothers and a senior-high community youth center. She had come to feel that she was God's partner, and she requested to be chairperson of the church board to help bring other church committees to life—and was excited about it.

—Several persons had found various parts of the regular worship service the source of their spiritual revitalization.

All the above examples illustrate experiences encountered on a pilgimage of growing maturity in spiritual formation. I suspect that most readers could think of someone they know whose spiritual life has been enriched in similar ways.

The thrust of the above is that the church in its corporate life needs to offer many experiences and contexts where members and others will have opportunity to become sensitive and aware of God's presence. It needs to be added that not only are there many different experiences that result in spiritual empowerment, but that there is an equal variety of behaviors evidencing this new spiritual vitality. When a person undergoes a vital spiritual experience, he or she will find appropriate ways of expressing it in witnessing, serving, and ministering.

IV. Increasing Lay-Clergy Teamwork in Ministry

a. The foundation for the empowerment of God's people to function in carrying out the church's ministry is *to be alive spiritually*. Since God reveals and speaks to persons in many varied ways, as just illustrated, the church must constantly seek to provide many contexts within which persons may become open and sensitive to God's presence and to vitalizing spiritual experiences.

Some contexts within which such experiences frequently occur include: corporate and/or private worship, working for social justice in the community, experiencing Christian love and fellowship, using one's talents in the church, Bible study, group sharing and discussion, ministering to the personal needs of others. The important point is that a church must not be restrictive and narrow to try to box in or limit the avenues to spiritual vitality through which God touches and renews the lives of persons, of groups, and of the entire church. Only as the church keeps its spiritual pilgrimage in the forefront of its life can it move towad a corporate ministry that expresses God's mission.

b. A second factor that will enhance lay-clergy teamwork in carrying out the church's ministry is *to seek consciously to identify the personal needs, goals, and abilities of members and relate them to the church's goals and activities.* Persons will get interested, involved, and committed to participate in the church's life when two conditions are present: (1) when what is going on is of importance and interest to them in fulfilling some of their own personal needs and goals while utilizing one or more of their abilities; and (2) when what is going on is of significance and importance as they understand what the Christian faith is all about. When a church is willing to take seriously the tasks of becoming sensitive to the needs, goals, and abilities of its individual members, and of providing activities and experiences of central significance in expressing *all facets* of the Christian faith in that community, lay and clergy teamwork will become a reality. Other chapters in this volume will deal in some detail with how this might come about.

c. Another factor that will contribute to increased involvement of lay people in the church's ministry is *their involvement from the outset in deciding what is to go on in the internal life of the church and in its outreach activities* as well. This would demonstrate a high level of respect and trust of laity both as persons and Christians. It would help interpret in an understandable and practical way the theological-biblical concept of the priesthood of all believers. This is not easy to do because it would require that the church deal openly with the great diversity of needs and values of its many members. A later chapter will seek to illuminate how such decisions can best be faciliated. However difficult, such lay involvement in the first stages of basic decisions of policy and programming are necessary to increase lay interest and participation in carrying out the policies and programs later.

d. Let us now suggest that the *clergy have a specific role in empowering lay-clergy teamwork* in the church's ministry. The pastor's leadership style, the quality of interpersonal relationships established, and the professional competence evidenced are critical factors in enhancing or blocking the empowerment of lay involvement in the church's ministry. We will carefully examine the pastor's leadership role in another chapter in relation to its effect upon lay participation in the church.

e. One final suggestion at this point for increasing lay involvement in the church is to develop a *comprehensive ongoing personnel plan for identifying, recruiting, training, and supporting lay persons as church leaders* that makes maximum use of their individual interests and abilities. This requires a concern for what working in the church does to and for the person as well as what it does to and for the church. Too often the church has no comprehensive plan to train and utilize members in its ministries and operates in a hand to mouth approach, pressuring or railroading persons into service to meet a church need. A carefully designed and implemented approach toward seeking to match persons and church needs in a way *that will be mutually rewarding* will be shared in another chapter.

V. Conclusion

Involvement of lay persons as co-workers with clergy in the church's ministry requires the vital spiritual empowerment of all persons involved. This necessitates an ongoing pilgrimage for all of God's people. The church must intentionally seek to provide many contexts in which sensitive, seeking persons may experience God's presence, gain increased understanding of God's nature and become deeply committed to doing his will.

Even spiritually alive persons (lay or clergy) require adequate resources and skills to enable them to witness and minister effectively. Some of these needed resources and skills will be dealt with in the following chapters in the hope of better "equipping the saints."

We see involvement in and service through the church's ministry itself as one important avenue to the spiritual empowerment of persons. Involvement in the work and ministry of the church may be the expression of faith for those who have become alive spiritually, or it may be the experience through which God may work to empower others spiritually—or both.

For this reason we are bold enough to move on to propose some specific approaches to facilitate increased lay involvment in the church's ministry in the chapters that follow.

Chapter 2

Releasing Human Resources

The "people power" of your church is its greatest resource—but recruiting, motivating, and directing lay persons is often a major source of frustration for church leaders. The church, as a voluntary organization, possesses three characteristics that often lead to frustration and poor results in channeling its people into effective programs. They are:

(1) diffusion of power;

(2) lack of accountability structures;

(3) absence of meaningful position-status rewards.

However, the members of the church represent a wealth of rich personal resources and motivation to volunteer time, talent, and finances to goals and programs.

Put these characteristics together and you come up with an organization confronted with a paradoxical complex of problems and potential; a maze of uncollected power, unused talents, and unrealized opportunities. Every congregation is confronted with the challenge to find means of channeling and turning loose its people power into areas of service that minister to the members and are responsive to human need. Such programming offers tremendous satisfaction to those who volunteer themselves to the church and its programs. In order for this to happen, however, the three characteristics mentioned previously must be understood and dealt with.

I. Diffusion of Power

In a for-profit organization or bureaucracy, power tends to be gathered around the "bosses" at the top of the hierarchical pyramid. These bosses control the power, releasing only certain amounts in ever decreasing quantities as it trickles down through the structure.

The local church, however, is not a profit-making organization or a bureaucracy. It is an association of volunteers owned by all the members, of whom each possesses a portion of the power. The bosses do not sit on top but are at the grass roots. They as individuals, choose to share their power with the leaders and programs they support, or to withold it from the leaders and programs they do not support. The task of every pastor is to gain and keep the trust and support of enough persons to "borrow" sufficient power to lead effectively. In this respect the members, all of them, are the bosses, and the pastor is a "power-broker," collecting the power from individuals and channeling it into programs and ministries they sufficiently support not to withdraw their power.

The power owned by each member comprises his or her ability to support or oppose, to attend or stay away, to volunteer or refuse to serve, to contribute finances or to withhold. The ultimate display of the member's ability to withdraw his or her portion of the power is the closed purse and the empty pew. The member who never attends and/or never contributes is exercising tremendous power. The member who loudly opposes the pastor and program at committee meetings, who causes so many frustrations and headaches, is not exercising nearly as much negative power as the disenchanted member who closes his or her purse and goes silently away. Few church leaders realize this.

II. Lack of Accountability Structures

Closely associated with the diffusion of power is the fact that in the local church there is little or no direct-line accountability. In the great majority of Protestant churches in America most, if not all, of the work done beyond that of the pastor is performed by members on a volunteer basis. In actuality the members are workers (volunteering services), clients (receiving services), and bosses (each one possessing a portion of the power) all at the same time. Whom then, do the volunteer workers answer to? The pastor? Not really, since he or she is not one of the member-bosses. Are they accountable to the administrative board? Not entirely, since the members of the board are church members, as are the volunteer workers, and as church members they all share equally in the "ownership" of the organization. Perhaps, then, the volunteer worker is ultimately accountable only to himself, or herself. Or put another way, perhaps every member is responsible for the life and ministry of the church. This is no doubt true, and where everyone is responsible, no one is accountable.

If the volunteer workers are accountable to no one, what then of the pastor? Is the pastor accountable to all the members, since all are "owner-bosses"? Whose interests and goals does he or she pursue when members' interests and goals are in conflict? The pastor's accountability is far more complex than that, however.

The pastor is associated not only with the local church (volunteer structure), but also with the ecclesiastical organization (non-volunteer, professional structure). Some agency beyond the local church passed on the pastor's qualifications for ordination; the pastor may be appointed to the local church by a bishop; somewhere in the ecclesiastical hierarchy is a board or person vested with the authority to review and possibly terminate the pastor's professional status in the church.

The pastor is the link between the local church (volunteer sector) and the hierarchy (non-volunteer). Whose interests, goals, and programs does he or she pursue when the interests of the local church and those of the hierarchy/denomination are in conflict? Because of this fuzzy accountability structure, pastors often develop their major allegiance to their own sense of integrity—an accountability that overrides all others. They become "Lone Rangers," responsible for everything but accountable to no one.

This lack of direct-line accountability in the local church is not all bad, for it creates an arena in which both laity and clergy can exercise creativity and equality. Unfortunately, it can also take its toll in organizational confusion, inefficiency, and ineffectiveness. To understand something of how this issue frustrates the church, one has only to observe the extent to which the church is generally unable to confront and/or terminate someone, volunteer or hired, who is doing an unacceptable job—secretaries who divulge confidences, board members who do not attend meetings, Sunday school teachers who do not prepare for class.

In order to improve the quality of the church's ministry and to enable the volunteers to experience success and satisfaction, the pastor must attack head on this matter of lack of accountability in the local church. The lines of accountability may never be perfectly clear, but much can be done to build support for and commitment to the kind of accountability that is necessary to harness and direct the people power of the church into effective ministries.

III. Absence of Meaningful Position-Status Rewards

Volunteers, of course, do not want financial remuneration for their services. Yet the absence of any meaningful rewards directly affects the volunteer's motivation to work. Even in the local church the volunteer must receive a meaningful reward or payoff for services rendered, or enthusiasm and effort will wane. This is a reality dilemma affecting every volunteer organization.

Many voluntary agencies (e.g., Alcoholics Anonymous, the school board, trustees of institutions, United Fund) are more willing and adept in offering meaningful, nonmonetary rewards than is the church. For this reason many enjoy more member-loyalty and volunteer commitment than the church.

Perhaps the church has erred in attempting too much to provide monetary rewards. Often the most visible jobs filled by part-time persons are rewarded monetarily (paid organists, choir directors, receptionists). We suspect this has done much to make all other part-time volunteers feel second-class, since the reward system treats them differently. Such monetary rewards cause motivational problems even for those who receive them, since the church generally cannot afford to pay what their time is worth to themselves or their families.

In the absence of a monetary reward system the church must provide spiritual, emotional, and honorific rewards in order to capture and sustain volunteer commitment. These rewards must be meaningful and personally satisying to the recipient. What is meaningful and satisfying to one volunteer may be empty of meaning to another. You have probably heard the motto, "Different strokes for different folks." It applies here.[1] Perhaps the single most important key to unleashing the vast resource of people power in your church is to provide meaningful, appropriate rewards for each and everyone who serves in any volunteer capacity.

These three issues—the diffusion of power, the lack of accountability structures, and the absence of meaningful reward systems—are major frustrations in the volunteer sector of the local church. Each of these issues, especially the latter, is important enough to become the theme of a separate manuscript. For now, however, we want you only to be aware that these issues exist and significantly affect motivation, decision-making, and programming in your church. To be unaware of them does not mean they are not issues in your church. To ignore them does not mean they will go away. Every pastor would do well to understand these issues and to control them; to turn them into resources rather than experience them as constraints, or at least to minimize their constraining influences.

So far in this chapter we have discussed certain issues unique to volunteer organizations which, unless managed effectively, will frustrate all efforts to recruit and motivate volunteer workers in the local church. Now we move to discuss the importance of the pastor's role in empowering lay persons for the church's ministry.

IV. The Pastors Role in Releasing People Power

The church comprises laity and clergy of various theological persuasions and program interests. This pluralism presents the pastor and leaders with their greatest opportunity to actualize all the potentialities resident in the congregation. For each member's potential will be developed only as he or she finds a service opportunity that interests and motivates him or her to work in it, to grow, to receive new training in order to be more effective, to carry new responsibilities. One reason many members are uninvolved and unwilling to take a job in the church is that the types of programs being offered are too narrow to represent the kinds of service opportunities they are interested in. It is safe to assume, however, that every member has some interest in serving God and the church or else he or she would not be in the church. It is a mistake for any pastor to build a church program that reflects only his or her theological position and program biases, or those most popular in the denomination. Such a program will leave many members who do not share similar interests uninvolved and stunted in their own development. These persons may leave the church altogether or seek out another church whose programs are more similar to their interests. In order to activate all the people power in the church, the pastor must seek to provide a wide variety of program service opportunities to which individuals and groups can commit themselves in keeping with their own Christian experience and interests.

Building church programs that allow for a pluralism of interests not only give members expanded opportunities to work and grow in their Christian experience, it also greatly expands opportunities for the church to minister to human need.[2] It is by attempting to minister to all the realities of human life and social systems that the church can realize its own full potential, as can the individual members who are in it.

In order for the church to minister effectively to a broad spectrum of human needs and to remain viable in its own environment, the pastor must possess the necessary skills to create and sustain effective plurallistic organizations. Perhaps a major barrier to pastors' becoming more skillful in this area is the pressure, both overt and subtle, to have every local church within a denomination pursue the same priorities and to organize alike, according to a plan set forth in the church's ecclesiastical law.[3] Ecclesiastical law, however, is not written to motivate and turn loose the power that is resident in a congregation; rather it is written to maintain denominational identity and keep order (and there is nothing so orderly as a corpse).

If your church is to do anything more than worry about its own maintenance and survival, it must set realistic goals, plan its own programs, create effective organizational units based on those goals and programs, recruit and train volunteer workers based upon their own interests, and manage the conflicts that will naturally arise in a church that is alive and constantly altering its goals and structures in order to utilize its resources most effectively in the light of ever-changing interests and opportunities. The pastor is largely responsible for creating the kind of climate in which this can happen.

V. Conclusion

These, then, are some of the issues that must be faced in attempting to motivate and sustain volunteer workers:

1. The diffusion of power
2. Lack of accountability structures
3. Meaningful rewards
4. A variety of service opportunities.

The pastor's own skill and attitude are crucial in all of these. The pastor alone cannot empower the laity for effective ministry. He or she can, however, effectively block all such efforts made by others.

Empowering lay people for the church's ministry requires management functions that fall largely to the pastor to see that they are done. We will deal with several of these in the chapters which follow.

The rate of change in our time is so swift that an individual of ordinary length of life will be called upon to face novel situations which have no parallel in the past. The fixed person for the fixed duties, who in the old society was such a godsend, will in the future be a public danger.

Alfred North Whitehead
1861–1947

Chapter 3

Appropriate Leadership Styles

If members are to be equipped for the church's ministry (Eph. 4:12), the pastor must assume primary responsibility. The scriptures are indeed clear that the church is given a ministry in which all members are to share corporately. This is precisely what the concept of the priesthood of all believers is about. Such an increased participation of lay members in the leadership of the church, however, will require changes in leadership roles for both clergy and laity.

I. The Dynamics of Lay Empowerment

Any change in member involvement must deal with the interaction of pastoral leadership and member response. Such changes are at once challenging and threatening to both, creating several possible tension areas.

A. Role Assumptions

Pastors may have ambivalent feelings about increasing the power of persons as co-workers. On the one hand, pastors may desire increased lay participation. Theologically it "fits," and practically it increases the programs and services the church can offer. On the other hand, it also requires that the pastor function in ways that may be new and uncomfortable e.g., he or she must share decision-making, provide quality training of workers, and function in a supportive and supervisory capacity. Working with laity as co-workers is different from assigning them tasks to do. We believe that a key factor blocking increased lay involvement is the pastor's reluctance to let go of the control of the church.

Consciously or unconsciously, many pastors interpret increased lay involvement as a decrease of their control, and that is threatening. This was illustrated in a seminar I led involving pastors from several denominations. We were discussing the theological meaning and practical implications of the concept of the priesthood of all believers. A pastor of the Friends congregation said he felt that the members of their church had as much responsibility to pray in the worship service, visit in the hospital, minister to the dispossessed, and speak in the Sunday service as he did as pastor, and that they so functioned. He indicated this is how he understood the meaning of the priesthood of believers. A pastor of another denomination arose with an ashen face and trembling voice, pointed a finger at him, and said, "My God, you don't believe in the priesthood of believers, you believe in the layhood of priests—you've just nnfrocked me." Changes in role assumptions evoke deep feelings that need to be recognized and faced.

Lay members also experience varied and ambivalent feelings about their increased participation in the life of the church. Some desire to keep their spectator role and fear both the time demands and skill training required for increased participation. These laity resist and are threatened by a role change to "activate" them. Other laity, who desire increased participation in the church's life, also experience anxiety about their changing role. Some fear they will be overwhelmed by responsibilities they are not yet ready to assume. The church's track record in lay training is not good. Some lay persons sense the clergy's resistance to their increased power on church boards, on both the local and national level, and this makes them uneasy. Many simply accept the status quo, having been reared in an atmosphere of high respect for clergy; they feel a "mystique" about pastors, and assume that only they can or should do certain things.

Past experiences and deep personal feelings, provide much dynamic material that will surface as role changes for both pastors and laity take place. Even when pastors and members both seek such changes, their deep inner feelings make the process very difficult

B. Ownership Assumptions Are a Source of Tension

Frequently, members feel the church "belongs" to them and the minister is their transient employee. They stay—the pastor moves. They "stake out" a "claim" on certain areas of church life that "belong" to them. They talk about "our church." They become very protective of "their" traditions, developed by persons whom they respect highly. Proposed leadership role changes in any of these areas of church life immediately elicit strong resistance and produce great anxiety.

Such lay persons expect the pastor to have certain specified areas of responsibility (i.e., preaching, praying, evangelism, calling, administering sacraments, weddings, funerals). They want the pastor to function in those spheres only and stay out of "theirs" (i.e., finance committee, trustees, Sunday school, women's work, board decisions). Any leadership style that calls for mutual decisions and a co-worker relationship involving the pastor in the finance or trustee committee decisions, or laity in calling or evangelism, may threaten "ownership" of various segments of church life. Any change in leadership roles and styles is anxiety producing and affects behavioral response.

Pastors also experience tensions relating to ownership assumptions. Many pastors refer to "my church" in a possessive context, and this is not merely a slip of the tongue. This "my church" syndrome is reflected in the behavioral leadership performance of the pastor. Such pastors insist on reshaping a church according to their own interpretation of what a church should be and often utilize an autocratic leadership style to bring it about. Tensions over ownership of the church surface when the pastor's my-church syndrome and the members' our-church assumptions come to a head. The question of whose church it is can be faced only as both parties acknowledge that it is God's church, and clergy and members alike are his servants. This basic problem of human self-centeredness must be acknowledged and worked through as clergy and laity seek to establish leadership styles that lead to their mutual involvement in God's work.

C. Hope for Bridging the Clergy-Laity Gap

A positive dynamic is emerging that holds hope for bridging the clergy-laity gap. A growing number of pastors and church members are committed to find ways to empower, train, and utilize more laity in significant roles and positions in the church. The Second Vatican Council gave a strong emphasis to greater involvement of laity in many areas of church life. This has resulted in the establishment of parish councils where laity are assuming increasing leadership roles in the Roman Catholic Church. In many Protestant denominations laity have been placed on the key policy and decision-making boards in significant numbers of the judicatory as well as local church levels. This trend is opening up many new areas of leadership for women as well as men in the church. New opportunities for clergy and laity to work together on bridging the gap that exists between them are arising. Together they are making decisions about such key issues as the nature of the church, a definition of ministry, determining new programs in a complex and changing society, and reshaping the church to meet today's needs. All these concerns involve developing new leadership roles and styles required to facilitate the increased use of laity in the work of the church today. There is hope that out of the increasing mutual involvement of laity and clergy together in these many levels of the church, communication channels will be opened and the Holy Spirit will empower the church for its task.

Change never comes easy. It always requires leaders who are facilitators of action and new patterns of behavioral response. Mindful of the dynamics of lay empowerment identified above, we turn now to explore leadership roles and styles that can be facilitating or blocking in regard to enabling increased lay involvement in the life of the church.

II. Implications of Leadership Styles

Organizational research indicates that a change in leadership style has a predictable cause-and-effect relationship to organizational outcomes and behavior.[1] This means that the style of leadership of the pastor and/or lay leaders is reflected in membership response; influences the members' patterns of interaction, involvement, communication, and support; and determines the outcome of members' activities. It is therefore important that careful attention be given to developing appropriate leadership styles.

We would define leadership as the enabling or influencing of persons and/or groups in the achievement of *their* goals. "Leaders accomplish their work through other people, and their success as leaders depends upon their ability to enlist and maintain follower commitment and collaboration for the attainment of group or organizational goals.[2]

Leaders display a variety of behavioral styles. The same leader may function differently in different groups, and even at different times in the same group. It is important that a leader be consciously aware of the style of leadership being used, why it is being practiced, and the effects of that type of leadership on the group. An awareness of the effects of one's leadership style will be useful to both clergy and laity. We will briefly share certain research findings regarding leadership styles to enable each reader to check out his or her own style. We will then suggest criteria for determining an appropriate leadership style for a given situation.

Should you see yourself or your church organization in the following vignettes, it is not coincidental.

A. *Leadership Styles from the Perspective of Decision Making and Authority*

One way of understanding leadership styles is by analyzing how decisions are made. The leader, in most cases, is influential both in *who* makes decisions and in *how* the decision-making process is carried out. A scale of decision-making, relating to leader authority and group freedom, diagrammed below, will help you identify your own way of functioning.[3]

Continuum of Leadership Behavior

Use of Authority by the Leader
Area of Freedom for Members

Leader makes decision and announces it	Leader "sells" decision	Leader presents ideas & invites questions, then decides	Leader presents tentative decision subject to change	Leader presents problem, gets suggestions, makes decisions	Leader defines limits, asks group to make decisions	Leader permits members to function within defined limits

The diagram indicates that the authority and control of the leader decrease as the area of member freedom increases. To move from one point to another on the continuum involves a change in leadership style. It also involves an increase in the involvement and freedom of members to participate in discussion and to influence the decision-making. The leader has several behavioral options from which to choose.

It will be helpful for you to place yourself on the chart at the point best describing your usual leadership style.

It will be even more helpful to ask the members of the group to place you on the chart to check out your self-perception. You should then reflect on what style might be more appropriate and why.

Personal Implications. As you think of yourself in relation to the above diagram, you will probably recognize one style that you use most of the time—it feels most comfortable or natural to you. You will probably also be aware of other styles that you utilize on occasion. For example, a participative leader may become more authoritarian if time pressure for completion of the task becomes strong, if a crisis arises, or if the particular group (perhaps a new one) is unable to function well with a participative leadership style because it is used to a different style. When a participative style is not resulting in the assumption of responsibilities by members of the group, the leader may shift toward a more authoritative style by seeking to set up circumstances that force the group members to assume responsibilities in order to achieve the original goal.

It is important for a leader to be aware of the style being utilized, to have selected it consciously, and to strive for flexibility. Leaders should be able to change styles when necessary because of the goals of the group, the maturity and skills of the group, the membership's history and traditions, or the time required by the task.

B. *Viewing Leadership from the Perspective of Concern for Persons and Task Achievement*[4]

Task achievement in any organization must be carried out by people. One way to view leadership is to discover how it prioritizes the concern for task achievement and concern for the needs of persons and their development. A helpful grid has been developed to identify leader behavior in these areas and is useful in exploring alternative behaviors available to leaders.

The Grid₈'s nine-point scale facilitates a visual measurement of a leader's concern for getting a task done *and* for what is happening to persons in the process. Task achievement and concern for persons in the group are both important. The intersection of these two measurements pinpoints the performance and emphasis of the leader. The leader can then check out other positions on the Grid more in line with his or her leadership goals and the needs of members. The Grid reproduced here represents five different theoretical positions or leadership styles.

MANAGERIAL GRID[5]

Not to be reproduced without permission.

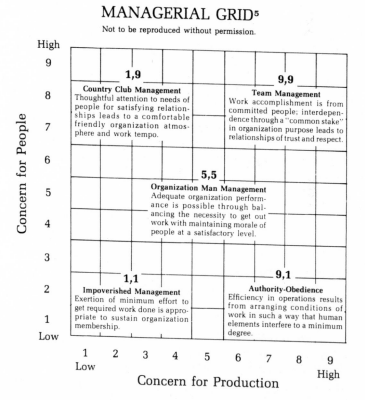

Concern for People (vertical axis: Low 1 to High 9)
Concern for Production (horizontal axis: Low 1 to High 9)

1,9 Country Club Management
Thoughtful attention to needs of people for satisfying relationships leads to a comfortable friendly organization atmosphere and work tempo.

9,9 Team Management
Work accomplishment is from committed people; interdependence through a "common stake" in organization purpose leads to relationships of trust and respect.

5,5 Organization Man Management
Adequate organization performance is possible through balancing the necessity to get out work with maintaining morale of people at a satisfactory level.

1,1 Impoverished Management
Exertion of minimum effort to get required work done is appropriate to sustain organization membership.

9,1 Authority-Obedience
Efficiency in operations results from arranging conditions of work in such a way that human elements interfere to a minimum degree.

Personal Implications. To rate your own leadership style from this perspective you might place an "X" in the square on the Grid where you think your concern for task and your concern for persons intersect. Next, ask each member of the committee or group of which you are a leader to do the same. This will give you a chance to discover how your own perception of your leadership style checks out with the perceptions of members of the group. To increase the effectiveness of your leadership and the functioning of the group, a serious discussion of the Grid should follow. In this discussion it is helpful to cite specific illustrations of leader behavior that lie behind each rating on the chart.

C. The Interactionist Approach to Leadership[6]

Leadership and membership behavior are interrelated, and neither can be understood unless so viewed. A basic concern of leaders must be how they relate to and work with followers (co-workers). Two factors are of basic importance in leader-member interaction: (1) mutual expectations between leaders and members, and (2) the quality of leader-member relationships. You will need to examine yourself in relation to each of these areas in assessing your leadership behavior.

1. *Mutual Expectations Between Leaders and Members.* One factor influencing the leader-member interaction is the mutuality of expectations and assumptions each has in relation to the other. For example, if the leadership style used is not one that is familiar or desired by members (e.g., authoritative or participative), a struggle will go on as the group seeks to change the leader's style to meet their expectations and the leader seeks to get the group to accept his or her style. This will consume most of the time and energy, and little task achievement will take place.

Another significant area of interaction is the relationship of the personal goals of individual members and the goals of the organization (which the leaders seek to achieve). When members feel their personal needs and goals are being met while they are pursuing the goals of the organization, the commitment and relationship to the organization (and leader) is strengthened. When group members feel that their personal needs and goals are ignored, or are contradictory to the goals of the organization, their reaction may take the form of absenteeism, withdrawal, refusing leadership requests, reduced financial support, and critical attacks on leaders and/or the organization. This is evident in church and all volunteer organizations.

2. *Quality of Leader-Member Interaction.* The quality and nature of the relationship between leader and members is critical. The quality of the relationship refers to the mutuality of the degree of genuine respect, trust, openness,and confidence between leader and members. Such a quality relationship will result in a high degree of commitment and collaboration between leader(s) and members in organizational goal achievement. Since leaders can accomplish their work only through other people, it should be clear that their ability to secure members' commitment and involvement is essential for their success. Research verifies that fact. "Based on several studies, leader-member relations emerged as the most important factor in determining the leader's influence over the group."[7] Interaction of leaders and members must be considered in assessing and seeking to develop an appropriate leadership style for any particular group.

The leadership research summarized here has much to contribute to church leaders who seek to increase the effectiveness of their leadership style in order to increase lay involvement in the church's ministry. You should now be aware of the leadership styles you are using and be able to check your perceptions with members of groups with whom you work.

III. Selecting an Appropriate Leadership Style

We now move to the pragmatic question of identifying criteria for determining an appropriate leadership style for a given situation. Anyone who has ever functioned as a leader recognizes immediately the difficulties and complexities in selecting the "right" leadership style. We believe the guidelines suggested below will be of help to ministers and lay leaders in finding appropriate styles for various groups.

First of all, we suggest that no one style of leadership is best for leaders in all situations. If the church is on fire, or a group member has suffered a heart attack, direct, authoritative leadership is called for. Such situations are not the time for small-group participative decision-making. Likewise, when a church in a rapidly changing neighborhood is doing goal-setting and long-range planning, that is not the time for the pastor or lay chairperson of a committee to send out an announce-ment stating he or she has determined what is to be done. That situation is one calling for board participa-tion and member discussion. There are myriad situa-tions in the life of a church in between these two extremes. For example, a group dealing with a task that is unfamiliar will need a great deal more structure and direction from the leader then will a group that knows its task very well. A leader needs to have a broad range of styles at his or her disposal, and to be able to match these with the needs of the group.[8]

Actually, the critical factors in selecting appropriate leadership styles are: (a) the range of different styles within which leaders can function, given who they are and the skills they possess, and (b) the maturity or immaturity of the groups with whom they are working, given the group's background and their ability to accept responsibility.

Lay and clergy leaders do have the opportunity to bring about significant change in the church by focusing on their own behavior. The style of leadership used in a given situation does matter. There is a cause-and-effect relationship between leader performance and its results which is predictable. Extensive research by Rensis Likert has identified six specific causal factors in leader performance relating to organizational vitality. These leader behavior charactistics have been researched in churches by the Center for Parish Development, which reports: "It has been found that when the leadership causal factors are combined with biblical understanding of ministry and mission of the church, they are key factors in bringing about productive cause and vitality in church organizations"[9]

The key causal factors of effective leadership are:

1. *Personal Support by the Leader.* When members preceive that the leader has a genuine appreciation of their personal worth and of their importance, as well as patient concern for their welfare, a sense of trust emerges. This opens communication channels, increases the willingness to risk new ventures, and a spirit of cooperation.

2. *Receptivity to Member's Ideas.* This style requires being easy to talk to and listening to what others say. It involves seeking out and using the ideas of others. Such a stance will result in a reciprocal seeking out of the leader to volunteer ideas. This markedly increases the input of ideas for problem-solving or planning, and greatly enhances ownership of decisions.

3. *High Performance Expectations and Personal Needs.* When quality performance is expected from members and is given by the leader, members catch the spirit and respond in kind. When a concern for high task-achievement is coupled with a concern for the personal goals and needs of individuals, members will participate with a high degree of interest, enthusiasm, and excellent results.

4. *Team Building.* Most effective organizations rely on team or group performance to achieve their goals. The leader can do much to establish a collaborative style of team functioning through a climate of open and honest sharing of ideas and feelings. In such a setting the goals set, decisions made, and actions planned by the groups affected are more likely to seem important and worthwhile. Creativity is encouraged in such a setting.

5. *Helping Members with Their Work.* Members respond to a leader who takes specific steps to help

them do their jobs better and more easily. Such leaders do not abandon them to carry out responsibilities any way they can. Rather, the leader enables performance through assistance in; (a) planning and prioritizing, (b) securing resources and training needed, and (c) support and helpful ideas during the implementation process. Such continuing interest and support stimulates motivation and enthusiasm. When this happens, these workers and other potential workers will be more likely to accept new responsibilities in the future.

6. *Involving Members in Decisions Affecting Them.* When members are involved in decisions affecting them, they feel a sense of importance because they are being taken seriously. This engenders a sense of confidence and support for the leader, and mutual trust develops.

We have been quite specific in identifying how a leader's behavior affects member response and creates changes resulting in a more vital church. This is true of the pastor's leadership of the church or lay leadership in various committees and groups. Other factors affecting change include: (a) a clear mission identification, (b) a facilitating structure and organization, and (c) a supportive organizational climate. All of the above need attention, but they can best be initiated through empowering lay and clergy leadership.

A change in leadership style is a causal factor in changing member response and vitalizing a church. One reason for this is that members reflect the leader's behavior. Members respond to one another in the same ways the leader responds to them. The style of the leader sets the pattern for member interaction in communication patterns, interpersonal relationships, norms of group behavior for expectations and goals.

If you examine your own leadership style in relation to the six factors just discussed, you may be able to pinpoint some areas where you might want to change your style. If so, read on, as we will deal now with what is involved in changing one's style of leadership.

IV. Changing Your Leadership Style

Supposing you desire to make changes in your own leadership style, how would you go about it? Keep in mind that abrupt and drastic changes in leadership style are usually unproductive. Such changes take time and are more effective when moved into gradually. This is true because leaders need both training and experience to acquire the needed skills to change their leadership behavior. The same holds true of group members, who not only must adapt to a new relationship to a leader, but also must learn how to assume their own new roles as members. This means that gradual changes toward identified directions need to be introduced in steps. Otherwise frustration and failure are likely to be experienced.

The six causal leadership factors identified previously might well serve as the directions for change by church leaders seeking to increase lay empowerment in the church. To actually move in this direction will take genuine commitment, training, and practice to acquire the skills needed and the attitudinal changes required.

Leaders will have to assess their "natural" or accustomed style of leadership in relation to these new performance goals. This will involve examining their own self-images, their value systems, their assumptions about group members, and their own feelings of security or insecurity. This is no small task. In addition, leaders will need to check out their skills and abilities in relation to those required to effect the six causal factors of leadership in organizational changes. Every leader will need to secure training in some areas of leader performance and will need to find opportunity for experience in the new roles. Training in leadership skills is available from many sources today, including church judicatory agencies, theological seminaries, continuing education programs, training consultants, management seminars, and various centers. Each leader will need to assess his or her own personal needs and embark upon an appropriate training experience.

Beyond these training experiences, leaders will need practice with feedback in becoming sensitive to the structures of each group with which they work, as well as to the time pressures, the abilities and skills of group members, the available resources, and the nature of the problem at hand. These are some of the factors that make an immediate leadership style change difficult and suggest that gradual changes over a period of time is a more fruitful approach.

It is not possible to determine how much leader-member behavioral change can take place in a given time period. The authors' experience suggests that major changes in leadership style and the accompanying membership response will take from eighteen to thirty-six months, but the changes can be made with excellent results.

Chapter 4

Effective Decision Making

I. Introduction

Lay participation in the church is greatly affected by the way decisions are made and who makes them, as well as what specific decisions are made. If a church's corporate ministry is to be carried out effectively utilizing members as participants, it must give careful attention to the decision-making process. Some of the reasons for this are discussed below.

Decision making gives power to the decision makers to determine what the organization is to be and do. Whoever makes the key decisions charts the course for the institution and defines the activities as well as requirements laid upon members of the institution. A church that claims theologically to be the people of God and to function as a priesthood of believers must look carefully at who makes the crucial decisions about defining its ministries. Shared decision making by members will empower those members to action when those ministries are underway.

Decision making is the control center of an institution. Decision makers determine what programs and activities will take place and which ones are unacceptable. Control is exercised in regard to securing and allocating human and financial resources. Control is exercised over nondecision makers by setting norms and requirements affecting them.

Many functional problems that arise in the implementing stage of church programs as expressed in

51

nonparticipation and nonsupport have their origin in the decision-making process. Resistance often expresses itself in absenteeism, hostility, conflict, and finally withdrawal from the institution. Nonparticipants frequently raise questions about *who* made the decisions and *how* the decisions were made, as well as object to *what* decisions were made. Often the bottom line is *why* wasn't I involved in the making of the decision?

Many researchers of behavior in organizations have verified that a participative style of involvement in decision making contributes to a more effective involvement in carrying out decisions. Rensis Likert has established this fact in industry, and the Center for Parish Development, of Naperville, Illinois, has verified it through research in churches. For these reasons, we believe any serious endeavor to empower laity for greater involvement in participating in carrying out the church's ministry must carefully examine how the church can improve its decision-making structures and processes.

II. Who Makes Decisions?

The decision makers, whoever they are, hold control of the organization and/or its subsystems. Decision making involves both power and responsibility. This power brings with it accountability for decisions made. Decisions are required at several levels in an organization, and the selection of the decision makers ought to be made consciously in accord with the nature of the decision and its effects. If the corporate church is called to be in ministry, then the involvement of lay persons in decision making at all levels is important as they will be involved in carrying out the church's ministry.

We have found it helpful to examine who in fact does make decisions in a local church. In most churches there are seven types of actual decision makers:

1. *The Formal Leader.* The pastor or lay chairperson may in fact be the decision maker. This may happen

even though committee votes are taken. Many manipulative procedures are used to enable the chairperson to "control" the committee.

2. *An Informal Leader.* The designated formal leader, whether pastor or lay person, may be neither the real leader nor the decision maker. Some member may be so influential in a committee or a congregation that others bow to his or her decision. This "real" decision maker may gain power in a group because of respect, fear, tradition, financial position, social prestige, expertise in the matter at hand, confrontation, or manipulative skills.

3. *A Subgroup Clique.* A few members may become the decision makers of a group. This clique may consist of the formal leader and a few friends, or any coalition of group members. They may sew up the decision by pre-meeting agreements. Other members will resent meetings whose outcomes are cut and dried ahead of time.

4. *The Total Group Membership.* The members of a committee or group may be the actual decision makers. Such group decisions are usually made by vote or some form of consensus. The decision made is recognized as the decision of the members of the group.

5. *Outsiders.* At times other groups or persons may be the real decision makers. Strange as it may seem, the decision a group or committee is struggling with may have already been made externally. The involved group may (a) be unaware the decision has been made, or (b) be trying to make decisions that they have no authority to make. Outside forces determining the decision may include the denomination, an ecclesiastical official, a city ordinance, a changing neighborhood, or financial reality.

6. *Tradition, Past History.* Previous members of the group may have established such strong traditions that change is nearly impossible. The determining decision-making question for some groups is, Did we do this before? If the answer is no, this ends the matter. In this

case the real decision makers are the previous committee member and past traditions.

7. *No One (Decision by No Decision)*. When a group
refuses to make a decision, everyone becomes a
non–decision maker by default. To make no decision *is
a decision* and has future consequences. This is a form
of group decision making very frequently used.

It *is* important for an organization to be *aware* of who
is actually making specific decisions. Only then can the
question be raised whether the right persons or groups
are making specific decisions. In fact, reactions to
decisions are affected by *who* makes them as well as by
what the decisions are. For example, committee
members react and behave differently when the entire
committee feels they reached a decision that is theirs,
than when members feel the chairperson forced the
decision, or the pastor exerted undue influence, or a
clique within the membership manipulated them, or
one dominating member controlled the group, or some
outside force left them no choice, or they were locked
into past tradition. The greater the importance of the
issue to be decided, the more significant it becomes as to
who really makes the decision. For instance, if the issue
is local church merger with another congregation, the
question of who controlled the decision will engender
more intense behavioral reactions than a decision as to
where to have the bulletins printed.

Behavioral manifestations related to who the decision
maker is include: power struggles between persons
seeking control, interpersonal conflict, deadlocks in
committees unable to make decisions, and withdrawal
from membership or participation. Such behavior is
often expressed in the form of hidden agenda. For
instance, many discussions about what church-school
literature should be used are a cover-up for who is really
running the church school—Mrs. Smith, the superintendent, or Mr. Jones, the pastor.

We are indicating the importance of any organization
being aware of who the actual decision makers are in its

ranks. This is essential to know before designing more effective formal structures delineating who should be making which specific decisions. It will also indicate where increased lay involvement in decision making needs to take place.

III. How Are Decisions Made?

This section on how decisions are made in groups is presented for the following reasons: (a) to help groups identify the ways they actually make decisions at various times; (b) to describe what is involved in each decision-making method; (c) to indicate when each method is most appropriate; and (d) the possible consequences and implication of each method.

A knowledge of the above factors will help a group in choosing a decision-making method appropriate to the moment, the task at hand, their own history, and their organizational goals.

The writers are indebted to Edgar Schein[1], Richard Schmuck, and Philip Runkel[2] for several categories of decision-making methods. We have these combined these catagories with our own to make up the framework of decision-making methods that follows. The drawings that illustrate each category were developed by Alvin Lindgren and Dave DuBink when they were consultants with the Los Angeles County Health Department, where decision making was a primary concern. The drawings attempt to depict both the decision-making methods being used and the *feelings of each member of the group* about the method being used.

We will describe several decision-making methods, indicating when each is most appropriate and suggesting probable consequences of each. We believe you will be able to identify specific meetings in your church where each of these methods was used.

A. Decision by No Decision (Refusing to Make a Decision)

1. THE PLOP (Lack of listening and response)

Description. No one listens, responds to, or raises questions about others' proposals. Members ignore all suggestions of other group members because each has his or her own proposal to present. One alternative proposal follows another without really being heard or considered, making each presenter feel his or her suggestion has "plopped." It is as though all speakers had stuck their heads out of the window and simultaneously made their speeches. No one is really listening. Frequently the meeting ends with no descision being made and the floor of the room covered with "plops." Sometimes the last proposal made is accepted because the group is running out of time. When this happens the decisions often plop in the process of being implemented.

When Appropriate? The plop is not a very useful method of decision making. It precludes careful listening, and hence each unheard speaker feels rejected by the group. This process also blocks development of ideas, building on others' contributions, and examining the positive and negative factors of each suggestion. This method of rapid input of many possible solutions to an issue is appropriate *only* as a conscious first step in brainstorming alternatives to be later explored in depth as the group moves toward a decision.

Probable Consequence. Frustration of the members is the usual result of this method of decision making. This is sometimes expressed verbally and is frequently reflected in irregular attendance or withdrawal. The postponing of decisions brings different consequences with various issues, usually not of a positive nature. When a quick decision is made at the end of a meeting, its soundness can be tested only in action rather than by careful discussion in advance.

The **LOST QUESTION**

2. The Lost Question (Getting off the Track)

Description. The "Lost Question" involves getting off target during the group discussion and dealing with one tangential matter after another until the group gets lost and does not deal with the main question at hand. The main question may be lost if the group unintentionally gets tangled up in details and subpoints. The lost-question approach may at times be employed deliberately to confuse the group, postpone action for one reason or another, or to block action.

When Appropriate? This approach to decision making is not recommended. It is discussed here because it is so commonly used in church groups as well as other organizations. When decision-making groups become aware that they are "caught" in this process, they need to acknowledge that they are lost, change course, and get back on track by identifying what the real issue is.

Probable Consequences. An unfruitful, frustrating session resulting in much wasted time and no decision.

The TERRIBLE QUESTION

3. The Terrible Question (The Group Is Unable to Face the Question)

58

Description. This method is a specific form of the lost question. Here the group is unable to handle the question before them because of its highly emotional, volatile, and/or crisis nature. Frequently, issues that turn into questions too terrible to face are either perceived as survival issues or threaten top priority values of a group. In order to cope with the threat and keep from facing what may be devastating, a group will "lose" the issue in many, many devious ways. They will spend time on defining the issue, raising points of confusion, declaring there is no issue, insisting seven other issues must be cared for first and bringing up all seven at once, and so on.

When Appropriate? Almost never. The terrible-question approach to decision making is a refusal to face a painful reality. It is an attempt to bury one's head in the sand, to pretend the issue is not there or that it will go away by stalling.

Probable Consequences. As long as an organization refuses to identify the terrible question and face it by appropriate decision making, that organization is dysfunctional. It will have to face the consequences of the issue at hand unprepared.

Conclusion Regarding Decisions by "No Decision" Methods

Any strategy of "no decision" decision making needs to be a conscious decision that there are proper reasons not to make a decision at that time. When an issue is not clearly defined, when more information is required, when the timing is wrong, or when the group has no authority to deal with the question, are examples of situations where no decision at that time may be appropriate.

B. Decision Making by Minority (A Single Person or Small Group)

The BOSS

1. The Boss (Decision by Authority)

Description. When one person makes a decision for the group, it is in fact a decision by a minority even though the decision maker may be the pastor or the chairperson of a committee. This is true even when the structure delegates such authority and even though the group members are asked for their opinions. When such is the case, however, the feelings of the group are usually quite different from those aroused when the designated leader usurps decision-making power and dominates the group, making their decisions for them. A member of the group other than the chairperson, or a small subgroup, may also usurp the group's decision-making role.

When Appropriate? There are occasions when decision by "the Boss" is appropriate: (a) when groups set up a structure giving the chairperson decision-making authority in prescribed areas; (b) when crisis arises, such as a fire in the building; (c) decisions of a minor nature may be given to any leader by the group, i.e., ordering janitorial supplies, arranging a suitable meeting room. Actually, many minor decisions are best delegated to one person or a small group.

Probable Consequences. One-person decision making is efficient in the sense that decisions can be quickly and easily made. One-person decision making usually produces a minimum amount of involvement by the group, frequently resulting in low ownership and varying degrees of resistance. This is most clearly seen in low participation during the implementation stage. Another drawback is that the creativity of the group members is not discovered and utilized in the making of the decision.

2. The Railroad (Minority Decision by Manipulation)

Description. Railroading is one of the oldest and most frequently used methods of controlling decision making in a group by a few members. Railroading is a technique used by one or two or three persons which results in actions and decisions in a group, but these actions are taken without the real consent of the majority. It is most frequently used by one or two persons to catapult an unsuspecting group member into the office of secretary. One person often railroads a group decision on the process of how the group should work by saying something like, "I think we should each express how we feel about this issue, and my opinion is . . . " Thus the group is railroaded into a work *process* even though the group never made an actual decision on the matter. The resultant work process may or may not be helpful in dealing with the issue at hand.

When Appropriate? Never.

Probable Consequences. Members resent railroading, particularly those who are railroaded. Frequently hostility surfaces against those who do the railroading. The decision-making methods discussed up to this point are used very frequently, but are not very productive of decisions that are actually implemented and helpful.

C. Decision Making by Majority

Effective Decision Making

1. The Vote (Majority Rule)

Description. The most common method of group decision making is by majority vote of the membership. Our political history and our democratic culture have given this method prominence. It is the simplest method of clearly determining the decision of the majority of the members.

When Appropriate? It is clearly superior to all minority methods of decision making previously identified, when wide commitment is needed. It is particularly appropriate for large groups, especially when widespread discussion precedes the voting. Voting is also an appropriate method of decision making when a decision must be made within a limited period of time. An authoritarian, manipulative chairperson, however, can short-circuit discussion, as can a member who is a "Robert's Rules of Order" expert, making the process very undemocratic, polarizing, and frustrating.

Probable Consequences. It is surprising that decisions by vote are often ineffectively and inadequately implemented. A lack of commitment to and ownership of such decisions are frequent. Somehow, many who vote for a decision do not get involved in carrying it out, or do so reluctantly. The drawing above portrays the unhappiness and resentfulness often felt by the minority of voting members. These feelings are heightened when there has not been full discussion, or when manipulative procedures have been imposed by chairpersons or members. Decision making by vote creates a win-lose climate where losers are apt to regroup, work against rather than for the majority decision, and try to make a comeback and win on a future vote. One other liability of voting as a decision-making process is that it is not likely to elicit the full creative contributions of all members.

2. Decision Making by Consensus

Description. Decision making by consensus does not always result in the 100 percent unanimity and enthusiasm of all group members. The drawing above indicates that the group decision was arrived at after real struggle and pain. Consensus is an agreement by group members that they have fully discussed and explored the issues, every member has been able to speak and be heard, and all feelings about the issue and the process have been expressed. Given these realities of the situation, the group agrees that they have arrived at the best solution possible and all members will support it. Consensus is an open, collaborative negotiation process. It involves taking all persons and all alternatives seriously and agreeing on the best possible solution in that context. A consensus agreement includes a commitment to live with and support the decision. In a real consensus decision everyone has contributed his or her thoughts and feelings and feels he or she has shared in the final decision.

When Appropriate? Consensus decisions are very time consuming, very difficult, and sometimes impossible to obtain. This means that sufficient time to follow through on this method must be provided for from the beginning. Short time lines may preclude consensus decision making. In addition to sufficient time, consensus decision making requires that both the leader and the group be committed to stay with the process and that the decision-making authority reside in the group. Consensus decision making requires the possession of skills within the group to facilitate two-way communication, to deal with interpersonal relationships, and to cope with conflict. When such skills are not present, an outside consultant may be helpful.

Consensus decision making is more appropriate to small groups and committees than large ones. The larger the group the more difficult it is to secure the full involvement of all participants, and the time requirements also are extended unduly.

Consensus decisions are also more appropriate to some issues than others. Minor decisions, if commonly recognized as such, ought not to require group consensus. The kinds of issues important enough for consensus decisions are those relating to goals, policies, procedural decisions as to how the group works, and issues involving high personal investment and controversy.

Edgar Schein rightly points out that procedural decisions as to how the group works are important to all members and ought to be decided by consensus. These are the very kinds of decisions frequently made by the chairperson, or imposed on a group by one or two members. *How* a group proceeds to deal with issues affects, if not determines, the outcome. The processes by which a group is going to function must be clear to everyone, and this ought to be decided by consensus.

Probable Consequences. Decision by consensus assures a sense of participation and involvement on the part of all members. This usually results in a commitment to support the decision, once agreed upon. It also assures that all alternatives were considered, that the spectrum of feelings surrounding the issue have been uncovered, and that a realistic appraisal has been considered as to what is likely to be involved in carrying out the decision. In consensus decision making, conflicting differences arise early in the decision-making process and are dealt with. In other forms of decision making most of the coping with the conflict has to be dealt with following the decision and sometimes sabotages the implementation stage.

How skillfully consensus decision making is done will affect the consequences of the process. If communication has been open, if everyone feels he or she has been heard, if all alternatives have been fully explored, if conflicts have been kept in the open and examined, and if all members were really involved in the final agreement, then consensus decision making will facilitate implementation effectively. If these things were poorly done, if insufficient time was given, and if manipulation of members took place, then frustration and resentment will block any real consensus.

The 100% er

3. 100 Percent Unanimous Consent

Description. Total agreement in group decision-making rarely occurs; however, there always remains a possibility that upon certain issues the group will agree 100 percent. When there is complete agreement, the decision is quickly reached. A 100 percent agreement is a painless, joyous decision. However, to hold the 100 percenter up as a model of group decision making discourages diversity, challenge, and tolerance, and participation.

When Appropriate? A unanimous decision is certainly appropriate whenever all members of a group are truly agreed. Seldom should a 100 percent agreement be required. If the furnace gives out in January, a unanimous decision to replace it is highly likely—and likewise are contributions to pay for it. Many crisis needs may fall in this category. A 100 percent agreement could take place either by vote or in the consensus decision-making process.

Probable Consequences. Unanimous agreement should mean that there will be 100 percent commitment to support and participate in the action required by the decision. If it does not, then some votes were not authentic.

We have now discussed the main decision-making processes used by groups and committees. The reader probably belongs to groups that use one or all of these procedures at different times. The *beginning point* in facilitating more effective decision making is to become aware of how decisions are being made at present. It is hoped that the preceding discussion will facilitate that ability. The author's experience in working with many church groups indicates that most groups are not aware of how they actually do make decisions; they are not easily made conscious of their decision-making behavior; and they frequently need outside help if they are going to facilitate a change in their decision-making pattern.

IV. Selecting An Appropriate Decision-Making Process

We are now ready to propose some practical guidelines as to how a group or committee can deal with the questions of *who* should make decisions and *what* decision-making process is best suited to a given situation. These guidelines are "tools" for groups to use as they seek to improve their decision-making process.

1. *Gather information as to what decision-making processes are being used, with what results, and how members feel about them.* Try to become aware of what is going on, analyze the results, and seek responses from the participants. A group *can* consciously look at its decision-making process. This may not be easy, however.

A group may select an observer or a team of observers from its own membership to study how the members proceed in making decisions. Results should be reported to the group as a basis for discussing its own decision making. Some items observers might note are (1) The way members give ideas and opinions; (2) how other's contributions are sought; (3) how feelings are expressed; (4) how members listen and respond; (5) how clarification is sought; (6) how the group surveys or checks out where it is; (7) non-verbal gestures; and (8) how conclusions are summarized and tested.

The following decision-making matrix is an adaptation for a church governing board of an instrument presented by Schmuck and Runkel for school groups[3] The use of this form will help a group identify the role each member should take in decision making. Any group can make appropriate adjustments by listing its functions down the rows and the persons or roles across the top. The matrix is designed not to solve problems but to identify concerns, to pinpoint group discussion, and to aid in focusing on the real issues involved in decision making—the degree of involvement various persons or groups should have in making specific types of decisions.

DECISION—MAKING MATRIX FOR CHURCH ADMINISTRATION BOARDS

Functions About Which Decisions Need to Be Made	Pastor	Professional Staff Persons	Chairperson of Board	Committee or Board Members	Church Members	Members of Sub-committees
Determining Goals						
Developing Programs						
Deciding Operational Procedures of the Board Re: Its Meetings						
Assigning Responsibilities to Carry Out Decisions						
Budget Building and Spending						
Evaluation and Control						

Code for Filling In Matrix:

I = must be INFORMED
P = must PARTICIPATE
A = AUTHORITY TO MAKE DECISION lodges here

C = must be CONSULTED
V = VETO POWER

2. *A second criterion for deciding how to select a decision-making process is to consider the nature of the task.* Various situations call for different approaches to decision making. Technical decisions calling for professional skill and knowledge (e.g., selection of which pipe organ, which audio system to buy) need to be delegated to a small number of qualified persons. Policy matters, however (e.g., whether or not to have a pipe organ or sound system), call for broad participation. Issues involving deep commitment and feeling (e.g., mergers, establishing larger parishes, moving to a new site) require careful consideration, full information, plenty of opportunity for all members to express feelings and to examine all alternatives and make the decisions. Certain specific tasks (e.g., details of setting up the meeting, getting needed information, following through on an approved action) can and should be delegated by the group to one person or a small committee. The task at hand determines which decision-making process is most appropriate.

3. *Available time and the size of the group are also factors.* Time limitations and a heavy agenda call for a group to assess whether or not to use voting or consensus for decision making. Consensus decision making is time consuming. On the other hand, a voting process that forces decisions on very controversial and emotionally laden items without full discussion may gain an immediate decision and raise even larger future problems (e.g., polarization or ineffective implementation). The time factor and all its implications need to be taken into account when deciding on appropriate decision-making procedures.

The size of the group making the decision also affects the process. Consensus decision making is not well suited to a body of a thousand persons. Voting seems required in a group of this size, though sub-groups, small-group discussions, and various cross-sharing and report-back designs can multiply the involvement of the members. Small groups best lend themselves to consensus decision making, but issues and situations may call for other methods at times (e.g., delegating or voting).

V. The Importance of Lay Involvement in Decision Making

Since it is the church that is called to the ministry of carrying out God's mission, laity and clergy alike must share in defining that ministry and in planning the specific ways for carrying it out. This will be enhanced if decision making involves representatives of members and groups in the church at every level of decision making.

As a congregation sets out to think theologically and functionally about defining its purpose as it seeks to carry out God's mission to that church and community, lay and clergy need to be involved in making the decision. This participative involvement needs to continue on as wide a scale as possible as goals are set, program planning is done, organizing and implementation takes place, and the evaluation process is concluded. Many decisions must be made at every step; and how they are made, and by whom, will have a real effect on the response and end result.

The clergy have a special responsibility in facilitating a participative structure *and* style of decision making in the church. This is not to say that laity are not also responsible in this area. Pastors, by the nature of their office, are related to and exposed to all areas of church life and have a comprehensive view of the whole. Pastors, as professionally trained persons, have as one of their primary roles the enablement and training of laity.

Here are some specific ways in which pastors can facilitate better decision-making processes in the church:

    1. Be willing to "let go" of control in many areas of church life and actively encourage and train lay

persons to participate in decision making at all levels.

2. Help establish an open and receptive climate at meetings that encourage all persons to express themselves, raise questions, and to respect one another's point of view.

3. Encourage the examination of any structures needing change in order to maximize lay participation.

4. Assist groups to think theologically and biblically as they explore the issues and concerns at hand.

5. Help groups and committees to find the resources needed both to make and to implement their decisions.

6. Utilize to the full all lay persons whose experience and skills can be used to improve decision making in the church.

One final word: *The decision-making procedures used in the various church meetings are very closely related to what turns people off or excites them to committed involvement.* Their involvement from the beginning in deciding upon an activity or their noninvolvement until their money or time is needed to carry it out often determines their attitude and response. If your church is serious about increasing lay involvement, do not minimize the importance of decision making.

Who makes decisions does matter.

How decisions are arrived at influences outcomes.

What is decided is affected by the above and will determine the ministry of your church.

Chapter 5

Congregational Assessment

Congregational assessment is perhaps unexcelled as a means of empowering all the members to participate in the church's decision-making processes. We ourselves have observed and have received numerous reports of congregations' having discovered new hope and vitality through the assessment process.

As a decision-making process, congregational assessment moves from decision-making by a minority—the boss, the railroad—and avoids the win-lose syndrome of the vote. It is a decision-making process based upon the consensus method and facilitates a sense of participation and involvement on the part of all members.

A Definition

Assessment is intended to produce a descriptive statement of the organization's actual state of affairs—its strengths, its weaknesses, and its members hopes for the future. It is much like taking a "snapshot" of the organization to determine such things as the attitudes of members, statistical and demographic information about the organization and its environment.[1]

Congregational assessment is a public activity. The entire membership should be encouraged and have opportunity to participate. As such it is quite different from other methods of assessment in which only the leaders are involved or in which an outside expert comes in to conduct a study of the church.

Designing an Assessment Process

It really doesn't matter what procedures you use to conduct assessment as long as the results are valid and useful to the organization being assessed and all the members have been empowered to participate. In designing an assessment process it may be helpful to recall the Oriental story of the five blind men attempting to describe an elephant. The point the story makes is that each blind man, though experiencing and describing the elephant differently from the others, was correct in his description—correct because he was describing the elephant as he "saw" it from his particular vantage point. Each group or individual has a different vantage point from which to view the church and may therefore have a perspective that, while differing from all the others, is nonetheless valid and useful.

In order to gain the most valid "snapshot," the views of many groups and/or individuals are needed. A way to develop this snapshot is to plan a process by which these many varied views can be put together to provide a description of the organization.

Some tools you may use are: home meetings, statistical and demographic charts, "town" meetings or public hearings, group discussion in meetings or worship services, every-member canvass, telephone interviews, questionnaires.[2] These are only a few tools at your disposal. The point is to select the tools, or create new ones, which are most suited to the needs and interests of your group.[3]

Home Meetings

A possible approach might be to involve the entire congregation in home meetings with about fourteen members invited to each.[4] Persons are trained to

74

conduct the home meetings by leading the group in a discussion of three questions:[5]

1. What do you think are the strengths of our church; what do we have going for us?
2. What do you think are the weaknesses (or major problems) of our church; what is going against us?
3. What changes or additions would you like to see in the next one to five years; what are your hopes and dreams for our church?

Some groups prefer to add a fourth question:

4. How should we relate to our environment/community? What specific program suggestions do you have?

Statistical Information Team

Certain important statistical information will not be collected in the home meetings—membership, church-school and financial trends, age-sex composition of the congregation and community, and such. A statistical information team should be appointed to compile desired statistical, demographic, and other types of information which the home meeting discussions will not produce.

Compiling and Summarizing the Information

Each home meeting plus the statistical study will result in a broad and varied amount of information. This material is then combined into one assessment report.

We suggest this be done by having one leader from each of the home meetings and from the statistical team gather to:

1. Decide upon a list of descriptive categories under which all of the material can be placed.
2. Collect all the strengths, weaknesses, hopes, program suggestions, and statistical information that are comprised in each category.
3. Write a brief narrative summary for each category (each summary should be no more than one page in length).

4. A narrative description of the church is then prepared perhaps using the following headings: basic strengths of the congregation, basic weaknesses/concerns of the congregation, major issues confronting our community, financial support for our church, major feeling tones in the life of the congregation, changes members would like to see take place. (The narrative report should not be more than ten pages, double spaced.)

Reporting the Results

The categories, each with its own list of information plus the narrative summaries, should be printed and reported to the entire congregation and also to the program and administrative units of the church for appropriate program action. The results of the assessment are then used by the program committees to establish goals and plan programs for the first through third years.

Many churches choose to report the information to the congregation using the same home-meeting format as was used to gather the information. Other churches choose to mail the material to each member and conduct a public meeting to answer questions, receive new suggestions, and so forth[6]

Summary

The congregational assessment is an important means of empowering laity for the church's ministry. This is accomplished by:

1. Providing an opportunity for every member to participate in a significant and beneficial process by which the leadership of the church can listen to and act on their suggestions. In short, the assessment allows vital information to flow upward from a broad membership base.
2. Providing significant training experiences for several members of the congregation and provid-

ing them an opportunity to experience and celebrate a significant success by applying their training to an important church project.

3. Enabling the members to:
   a) generate valid information that they can understand about their church, its problems and opportunities;
   b) have an opportunity open to all to search creatively for solutions to the problems, to make free and informed suggestions and choices;
   c) Participate in a process that will increase their own commitment to the congregational plans and programs that are based upon the assessment data.[7]

The empowering aspects of the assessment are to be found in the open discussion by the members regarding the church's strengths, weaknesses, and future possibilities. With alteration of the process these issues can be discussed by congregations of twenty-five or twenty-five hundred members. Further, these questions can be used to foster assessment by organizations and committees as they seek to improve their own effectiveness within the church.

There is a principle worth remembering when conducting an assessment: "People tend to support what they have helped to create." About the only information that a congregation will really "own" and use to strengthen its programs is information that the congregation itself generates about the church and its environment. Ownership of the assessment information grows as members listen to one another. Comments like, "Hey, its comforting to know others think the way I do," or "That's a new idea I never thought of at all" are common indicators that support is growing for the information.

Every pastor has had the experience of reporting to the congregation information and/or priorities handed down by the church through its national and regional agencies. Often this information seems not to sink in, not to excite and mobilize the people for action. Until the members of the congregation own the information as their own, chances are they will ignore it, confute it, possibly even vote on it, but not act on it—and if they do act on it, the action is often taken halfheartedly or grudgingly. If you want your congregation to become excited about information, to use it with enthusiasm, then remember that people tend to be turned on by information they have helped to generate.

> Information is the key
> instrumentality to
> all change.

Chapter 6

Planning for Action

For want of a skilful strategy an army is lost; victory is
the fruit of long planning.

Proverbs 11:14 NEB

Said Alice to the Cheshire cat:
"Would you tell me, please, which way I ought to go
from here?"
Said the Cat:
"That depends a good deal on where you want to get
to."
"I don't much care where . . . ," said Alice.
Then, said the cat, it doesn't matter which way you
go."

—from *Alice in Wonderland*

BUT IT DOES MATTER

. . . at least for the Church . . .
. . . and particularly for *your* church!
Congregational assessment by itself is an empowering
process and can, upon the basis of the enthusiasm and
information it generates, be expected to produce
positive change in the church. It will, however, produce
greater benefits when the results are used to make
intentional program decisions and for planning the
future of the church. Assessment is a vital ingredient in
any successful goal-setting and planning process. We

move now to a discussion of the ingredients of a planning process that will further empower the laity for the church's ministry.

Recent years have seen churches and denominational agencies giving a great deal of attention to goal setting and planning. In spite of this, however, few churches have any sense of a unique mission or of specific objectives to which resources are being directed. As a result, many churches have survival as their major concern—to keep the doors open, the building in reasonable repair, and the bills paid. Others are not in such drastic circumstances. For them the goal is to get by and to get a little bit more of what they have—a few more members, a few more enrolled in church school, and income increases to keep pace with rising costs. Some churches, however, are experiencing the thrill of growth and challenge. These are generally those which have directed their resources toward the achievement of carefully established, realistic goals and, in the process, experience new life and power.

The cry of the church in the sixties was "let the world set the agenda." The world was altogether too willing to do it. The church abdicated a vital part of its mission and planning to external forces and became reactive instead of proactive. And in doing so it became scattered and dissipated in its rush to follow the world wherever it went. Now, in the eighties, the church is re-collecting and re-membering itself. A much used means to do this is the goal-setting process.

Planning the Future of Your Church

The question is not *whether* your church will have a future, but *who* will determine it. Will its future be determined by the environment, with its often indifferent and hostile attitudes toward the church, or by the members who love, care for, and support the church? As the environment continues to become more unpredictable and crisis-ridden, it will become ever more imperative that the church conduct its programs in a planning mode. This necessity presents you with a grand opportunity to further empower lay persons for ministry. Few programs or activities can significantly involve such a large percentage of your congregation as can a church planning process.

Planning is like navigation. If you know where you are and where you want to go, navigation is not so difficult. It's when you don't know the two points that navigating the right course becomes difficult. To illustrate this logic, let's use a comparison. Assume you board a luxury ocean liner, its engines already running in preparation to leave port. You go into the chartroom and ask the captain to show you on his charts your present location, what his next port-of-call will be, your final destination, and the route he is planning to get there, and he answers, "I really don't know any of that; I just pay attention to keeping the ship moving." Would you be confident of his reaching his destination? Would you want to be a passenger on his ship?

Should you not use the same intelligence in planning the future course of your church that you would reasonably expect of the captain? There has never been a church leader who planned to fail, but there have been many who failed to plan. Unfortunately the results are about the same.

The story of the captain points to three vital "points" the church must chart in conducting a planning process: where it is now, where it hopes to be at a future time, and the route it plans to get there. These can be diagrammed to illustrate a goal-setting and planning process (see diagram on following page).

Mission Clarification (Who Are We?)

Mission clarification is a theological process in which the congregation determines its missional values and prepares a normative statement of what it intends to be and do.

PLANNING CYCLE

Over the past several years some main-line churches have used the word "mission" in such a way as to make it synonymous with "activity," so that whatever a congregation or group does is seen as mission. We choose to draw a distinction between mission and activity, for we believe this approach to mission has caught many local churches and ecclesiastical agencies in an activity trap in which more and more programs and activities are engaged in with fewer and fewer beneficial results; a kind of activity merry-go-round on which the most serious missional question considered is, Well, what do we want to do this year?[1] and the measuring stick for determining this often is, "if it sounds interesting, do it."

Mission clarification is not meant to determine specific activities, but to ask the *why* of all activities engaged in. It is the church doing its theological homework to determine which direction will best move the church from where it is to where it ought to be. Goal setting tells "what and how"; mission clarification asks "why."

Mission clarification deals with the question of *purpose*, and should be a distinct, intentional step in the planning cycle whenever the group is unclear about its most appropriate relationship to its environment, or when the congregation is seriously questioning its future. If the group is not facing such issues, and if there is a clear degree of agreement regarding theological values and missional priorities, you may choose not to include this as a distinct step in the planning process.

For a more complete discussion of mission clarification, with suggested procedures, see our earlier volume, *Management for Your Church.*[2]

Congregational Assessment
(Where Are We Now?)

Congregational assessment is meant to develop a descriptive "snap-shot" of the church, its programs and environment. The assessment material becomes foundational for formulating goals and plans designed to make the entire church program more responsive to the needs and interests of the congregation.

It is a mistake for the clergy and lay leaders to assume they know the directions the members think the church should take, unless the members have been enabled to express their opinions on a broad range of subjects in a receptive, nonthreatening climate. Congregational assessment can offer such structures and opportunities.

Goal Setting (Where Do We Want to Be?)

Goal setting, based upon congregational assessment and mission clarification, is a prescriptive process resulting in a "how to" plan for the church which strategizes the activities and programs the group believes are most consistent with its theological values and missional priorities, and which are realistically achievable given its present "location" and condition. In the planning cycle, goals are seen not as the end product, but rather as targets or intermediate ends. They are achievements required to bring the church closer to its own theological-missional values.

In recent years denominational agencies have produced many resources to guide church committees in goal setting. Many of these resources share two common characteristics:

1. They fail to stress the fact that effective goal setting is only one step within a larger planning process. Goal setting must be preceded by organizational self-assessment and mission clarification, and followed by effective action planning (implementation) and evaluation.

2. They fail to stress the fact that the planning process should deal with the congregation as a system, and with all of its programs as a whole. A congregation can be empowered for ministry only by bringing all of its programs into a coordinated effort to achieve its mission. Goal setting that focuses on *segments rather than on the whole* will never bring a church to its full potential.[3]

Implementation (What Shall We Do to Reach Our Goals?)

Good implementation begins with developing a good plan. This plan needs to be written and comprehensive enough to serve as a "road map" to achieving the goals. A road map that is so incomplete as to leave out important information is no good, and one that is cluttered with unimportant and confusing material is also no good. A good implementation plan will give information regarding the following:

Strategizing: *What* activities will we do to reach our goal?

Scheduling: *When* will each activity take place?

Recruiting and Assigning: *Who* is responsible to see that it happens?

Resourcing: *What* are the equipment, space, money, and worker needs to carry out the activity?

Monitoring: *How* will we check up to be sure the plan is functioning properly and on time?

Strategizing

A good place to begin in developing action plans is to choose your route—the steps or activities to achieve the goal. Remember, just like a road map, there are always many "routes" you can follow to reach your destination, your goal. And each route may have many steps along the way. The routes you follow should be carefully selected, based upon people's interests, abilities, available resources.

You may choose to brainstorm many activities and then select those which seem most feasible. After you have decided upon the activities, the next step is to put them into sequential order, thus providing a list of activities and the order in which they will be carried out in order to reach the goal.

Scheduling

After the activities are chosen and put into sequential order, a calendar is developed showing when each activity is to be completed. If the list of activities is very long or complex, setting up a calendar can sometimes be a difficult task. A helpful technique is to first establish the beginning and ending points—the date activities are to begin on the goal, and the date when all activities are to be completed. Having established these two points, continue scheduling from the beginning point until reaching the point where you are no longer sure of dates, time needed to do a step, and so on. Then begin scheduling from the ending point back toward the front. Continue this until reaching a point of uncertainty. With this new information schedule, move some more from the front, then again from the back, and so on until both schedules meet in the middle.

Recruiting and Assigning

Having built the schedule, the next step is to recruit someone for each task to see that the job is done on time. Many church planning processes go awry at the points of scheduling and recruiting/assigning. They fail to clearly schedule each step, and/or they fail to assign persons to be specifically responsible to carry out each step.

Following are some rules that, if adhered to, should enhance your implementation efforts:

1. Remember! No one is assigned to any task until he or she has been personally contacted and has freely volunteered to do the task. To assign anyone to a task without first getting his or her consent is a sure road to frustration and failure. Such action often results in noncommitted workers who fail to carry out their responsibilities. If you should ever remind them of their responsibilities, they cry, "Hey, what do you expect of me? I never wanted this job in the first place!"

If any goal cannot readily generate sufficient volunteer interest to carry it out, it is safe to assume it never will be carried out and should be abandoned. This process is one means of deciding which goals are in fact priorities for the people.

2. Remember! Each step is assigned to someone who has agreed to be responsible for seeing that the step is carried out on schedule. That person is not necessarily responsible for doing the work, but he is responsible for seeing that it is done. He or she may likely have to recruit others to work with him or her.

A common tendency (pitfall) for church planning groups is to expect that the entire committee will assume responsibility for seeing all the steps are carried out. This is courting failure! When everyone is responsible, no one is accountable; and "let George do it" reigns supreme.

Resourcing

Asking someone to take a position, or to do some activity in the church, carries with it the moral responsibility for providing that person with the necessary resources to do the job well. Resourcing, therefore, becomes an important part of implementation planning. It does little good to plan a program if you will not have the resources to carry it out.

Resourcing involves determining and providing for such needs as equipment, space, money, volunteer workers. Resourcing needs for simple programs can be quickly identified. More complex programs, however, may require careful analysis and resource planning.

Monitoring

This involves determining how the entire plan will be followed to be sure it functions properly and on time. The earlier implementation steps of strategizing, scheduling, and assigning provide the framework for monitoring. Monitoring questions are:

1. Where are we in the plan, what steps are accomplished, and what should we do next?
2. Are the steps being done according to schedule? If not, what adjustments should be made to get the plan back on schedule?
3. Are the workers doing their job satisfactorily? Are they in need of resources? Do we need additional workers?

We suggest two principles to assure that the monitoring function is carried out in such a way as to help keep the program on target:

1. When preparing the implementation strategy, schedule check-up dates at crucial points to review the progress and results of the plan.
2. Appoint a goal manager whose responsibility is to monitor the entire plan. The goal manager is responsible for reminding persons of their assignments far enough in advance to ensure they have not forgotten. The goal manager also stays in close

"HANDY DANDY" PLANNING CHART

GOAL: Develop Effective
Evangelism Program

Steps/Strategies		June	July	Aug.	Sept.	Oct.
Recruit Evangelism Committee (Pastor)	P					
	A					
Committee Develop Plans (Committee Chairperson)	P					
	A					
Contact Local Churches for Facilities (decide later)	P					
	A					
Contact Prospective Training Leaders (Pastor)	P					
	A					
Decide upon and Order Materials (Chairperson and Committee)	P					
	A					
Publicity for Training Sessions (Chairperson, Pub. Task Force)	P					
	A					
Recheck Leaders and Facilities (Pastor)	P					
	A					
Conduct Three Training Sessions (Pastor)	P					
	A					
Evaluate Effect of Training Sessions (Evaluation Task Force)	P					
	A					
Ongoing Evangelism Activities	P					
	A					

"P" = Planned Schedule

"A" = Actual Schedule

Worksheet Prepared by: Administrative Board						
Goal Manager: John Jones					Date: 5/29/79	
Period Covered: 6/79—5/80			Review Dates: 1st Mon. each month			
Nov.	Dec.	Jan.	Feb.	Mar.	Apr.	May

PLANNING WORKSHEET

GOAL: Write goal in measurable terms, if possible: numbers, percentages, dates.) _____

DATE: _____

GOAL MANAGER: _____

CHECK-UP DATES: _____

What Steps Will We Take to Achieve the Goal?	Who Will Be Responsible for the Step?	When Is It to Be Done	What Resources Will Be Needed for This Step?	What Will the Result/ Product Be?

touch with workers, providing resources, helping solve problems, and spotting any potential break-down of the plan before it happens. If the goal manager cannot solve the problem, he or she will request help from the pastor, administrative board, or others.

Above are two worksheets to assist in implementation planning. You may choose one of these, or develop one more suited to your needs.

Evaluation (How Well Did We Do in Reaching Our Goals?)

Evaluation serves two important purposes: it helps monitor existing programs to identify needed changes while there is still time for the changes to make a difference, and it identifies new programs and activities which may be needed to help the church accomplish its mission.

Evaluation should be going on throughout the entire planning process and should be conducted in such a way as to allow all the members to offer evaluation, not just the clergy and lay officers.

Most church groups conducting evaluation do so by means of a questionnaire survey. Our experience is that this is perhaps the poorest method. People do not generally like to fill out questionnaires, having been conditioned to them in unpleasant situations—e.g., filling out income tax forms, standing in long lines during college registration, being admitted to a hospital when ill. It is not too surprising to discover patient and pleasant church members responding with lack of interest or hostility when confronted with question-naires from the church.

A generally better approach is to use evaluation methods that enable persons to communicate together in face-to-face settings regarding their opinion of the church program and to gather "hard" data regarding the programs. Such methods as small-group discussions, personal interviews, public hearings, and telephone interviews may be considered. As an aid to these methods, a questionnaire may sometimes be effective to facilitate and focus discussion so that the desired information is generated.

An Evaluation Guide

Following is a series of questions we find helpful in guiding church groups regarding the kinds of information they need to do good evaluation:[4]

I. Evaluation of Goals and Objectives
   A. What are the goals we have been pursuing?
   B. Are these goals consistent with our mission? Are they the right goals?
   C. Are the goals clear (do we know what needs to be done to achieve them?) and realistic (can we hope to achieve them?)?
II. Evaluation of Programs and Activities
   A. Is our program(s) consistent with our mission and goals?
   B. To what extent is our program(s) achieving its goals? Is it effective?
   C. Is our program(s) worth the time, effort, and money we are putting into it? Is it efficient?
   D. Are there any positive and/or negative side effects? Are our programs causing any un-planned, unanticipated results?
III. Problem Solving and Future Planning
   A. What changes need to be made in our present program to make it more effective in reaching our goals and mission?
   B. What new goals and programs do we need to help us achieve our mission?

Evaluation should be as much a "style" as it is a distinct activity. Distinct times and processes by which the church evaluates the effectiveness of its programs are important. Equally important, however, is to develop a norm in which it is okay for the congregation to ask how well its programs are doing, and to give and receive honest feedback.

In the church, evaluation is currently the least evident of the components of the planning cycle. Evaluation constitutes a "missing link" in many church planning processes because congregations and leaders are reluctant to measure the achievement of and feed back the results to, volunteer work groups. "How can we do this? After all, they are volunteering their time!" This attitude often has a reverse effect: "What we're doing must not be very important. After all, no one seems to care how well or badly we are doing." Helpful evaluation and feedback do much to improve program effectiveness.

Organizational Structures as a Means of Increasing Commitment

The organizational structures of the church are a powerful influence upon the degree of commitment the congregation will have to the goals it has established. Any strategy, therefore, to affect major positive change in the church should consider the alteration of existing structures or the creation of new organizational structures designed to achieve the new goals. *Form follows function!* Without new organizational structures, the goal-setting and planning process may not be fully effective. This is another step where many goal-setting and planning processes begin to go awry. It is not the failure to establish clear and realistic goals, but an unwillingness to discard or change the existing organizational and political structures which generally frustrates the members and results in too little commitment to carry the process through to goal achievement. Christ addressed this issue when he said, "Neither do you put new wine into old wine-skins; if you do, the skins burst, and the then wine runs out and the skins are spoilt. No, you put new wine into fresh skins; then both are preserved" (Matt. 9:17 NEB). When a church goes through the process of establishing goals without revising existing program structures or creating new facilitating structures, the new goals are often lost and the existing structures are weakened. The result is that both the wine (the new goals) and the old wineskins (the existing organizational structures) are made less effective.

Organizational Structures and "Sacred Cows"

One of the realities in many churches which mitigates against organizational change is a sense of sacredness that has been attached to the existing organizational structures. The structures have become sacred cows to be guarded and preserved at all costs. In such instances, form is not allowed to follow function, but is forced to follow tradition.[5]

Procedures to Be Avoided in Goal Setting and Planning

There are centain procedures that will not work in church goal setting and planning. Following are some processes to be avoided.

1. Goals that are established by the church staff and lay leaders and then submitted to the church members for ratification. Members today tend to support goals and plans they help make, not those made by leaders.
2. Plans that are legislated by superiors or denominational agencies.
   a. Just as members tend not to "own" those goals made by the local church leaders, so there is an increasing unwillingness on the part of clergy and of laity to "own" goals or plans that are handed down from above.
   b. In a rapidly changing environment it is very unlikely that any person or group outside of the local church can establish the best goals for the church unless they have personal, consistent relationships with the people and programs of the congregation.

3. Goals that are the result of a study conducted by a hired, external "expert." Every church is unique and exists in a unique environment. Therefore, its goals and plans, and the process for achieving them, must be a product of the congregation, not of an outside expert.

We are not saying that goals and plans cannot be made by the above methods. As a matter of fact, such methods are widely used. What we are saying is that these processes are generally not effective and are meeting with increasing opposition or lack of interest at the local church level. There are better methods. Some guidelines can now be stated for effective church goal setting and planning.

Guidelines for Church Goal Setting and Planning

1. Seek to involve in the entire planning process every member whose volunteer service, money, and support will be needed to implement the plans and achieve the goals.

2. Involvement of members means they will have decision-making power in setting the goals and in determining the structures that are needed to implement them. Also, they will be given opportunity to serve in the structures that are set up to accomplish the goals.

3. The function of the pastor and lay leaders is to enable the congregation to formulate realistic goals and plans. After the plans are formulated, the pastor and leaders assist the laity to establish organizational structures to implement the plans, and provide training and resources to equip those who are selected to carry out the programs. Leadership of this type empowers lay persons for the church's ministry.

Conclusion

Goal setting and planning processes that involve the congregation as a whole do, of course, empower the laity. This empowerment results in more member participation in decision-making and greater commitment to the ministry of the church. Speaking in favor of the kind of planning processes we have described, Dr. Thomas Gordon states:

No one is apathetic except in pursuit of someone else's goals. . . . People work hard to accomplish goals they set for themselves. But they experience this opportunity so rarely that you can expect a burst of enthusiasm when they are given the chance. People get sick of having someone else set goals for them, not because they resent authority, but because they have talent that is not being used. They want to exercise their [own] muscles. . . . People are happier when given a chance to accomplish more. A sense of accomplishment, the feeling that they have done something worthwhile, brings most people pleasure and a sense of importance. The more often they can experience these satisfying feelings, the more interested and enthusiastic they will become and the more they will attempt to repeat the experience. The challenge to you as a [pastor] is to see how often you can give [them] such opportunities.[6]

The church may enter the planning cycle at various stages. Once the cycle is entered, however, we suggest the process be designed to follow the steps as outlined in this chapter, and that evaluation be a part of every stage, measuring the effectiveness of that which has been accomplished and influencing that which is yet to be done.

Finally, the entire goal-setting and planning process is a cycle. No sooner is the process completed than it is time for the cycle to begin again. Perhaps a rule of thumb might be to establish a cycle of one- to five-year goals and plans, with an annual review to adjust, add, and delete goals and plans in order to make the entire program maximally effective and responsive to changes within the church and its environment.

> There once was a preacher
> Whose principle feature
> Was hidden in quite an odd way.
>   Lay persons by millions
>   Or possibly zillions
>   Surrounded him all of the day.

Planning for Action

When once seen
By his saintly bishop
And asked how he managed the deed,
　He lefted three fingers
　And said, "All you swingers
　Need only to follow my lead.

To rise from a zero
To a Big Parish Hero,
To answer these questions you'll strive:
　Where are we going,
　How will we get there, and
　How will we know we've arrived?"[7]

And that is what good planning is all about!

Commit to the Lord all that you do, and your plans will
be fulfilled.

Prov. 16:3 NEB

Chapter 7

Securing Responsible Leaders

The recurring theme of this book is that the church's ministry must be carried out by its members. In the previous chapter we described an action planning process, but it will be of no avail unless persons are enlisted and trained to give leadership to whatever is planned. A vital congregational ministry requires committed and skilled lay leadership. We now turn our attention to how such lay leadership can be challenged, secured, and trained to serve the church as it carries out its ministry.

The Basic Concepts Underlying Leadership Development:

1. **The New Testament Portrayal of the Church's Ministry as a Responsibility of All Christians.** The sharp division between clergy and laity that exists today is not evident in the New Testament. Every Christian is to be viewed as a priest, one of God's own people, responsible to "declare the wonderful deeds of him who called you" (I Pet. 2:9 RSV). The writer of Ephesians states that pastors are "to equip the saints [members] for the work of ministry, for building up the body of Christ [the Church]" (Eph. 4:12 RSV). We have expanded this concept in some detail in the opening chapter of this volume.

2. **A Vital Personal Faith Pilgrimage Underlies Acceptance of Leadership Responsibilities.** Persons with a vital, growing faith are increasingly sensitive to human and spiritual needs and give of themselves and their resources to meet these recognized needs. Such persons compose "the handful of the faithful" to be found in every congregation. They can be counted on to respond whenever needs arise. Increasing the number of persons experiencing a meaningful faith pilgrimage will provide more quality leaders to expand the church's ministry. This spiritual dimension undergirds all efforts to improve the quantity and quality of church leadership.

3. **A Church's Actions in Meeting the Diverse Needs of Its Members and the Community Will Affect the Willingness of Persons to Assume Leadership Roles.** As a congregation, what we do speaks louder than what we say. Our performance affects how persons respond to us as a congregation. If our programs and ministry contribute to the enrichment of the personal goals and needs of individuals and/or to community needs and issues high on their value scale, they frequently respond through leadership involvement on their part.

4. **Every Local Church Has an Untapped Potential of Human Resources and Talents.** The unused potential of human resources in every church is staggering. The potential is there, but it must first be identified and discovered, and then be harnessed and channeled into usable service. Every church has room to improve on the use of its human potential. This chapter is written to identify specific ways of releasing the power of these unknown or unused human resources.

5. **Persons Will Respond to the Challenge of Doing Significant and Useful Tasks.** Persons will not give of their time and ability unless they feel what they are doing is worthwhile and significant. Jobs must not be created just to keep people busy, or continued just because they have always existed. Churches must

seriously ask of every task, Is this really necessary for the achievement of God's mission and our ministry? We need to rethink what we are asking people to do, and why.

6. **A Comprehensive Leadership Recruitment and Development System Must Be Developed and Carried Out by the Nominating and Personnel Committee.** The actualization of the basic concepts enumerated above will depend upon the establishment of a functioning, ongoing nominating and personnel committee. This committee will need to carefully design and carry out a detailed and comprehensive program for identifying, motivating and enlisting the potential leadership of the church, and to provide the training and supportive supervision needed for their effective functioning.

7. **The Pastor Plays a Key Role in Both the Securing and Training of Leadership.** The role of the pastor as a developer of leaders is twofold. The pastor facilitates motivation and enlistment of lay persons for leadership roles through increasing the spiritual vitality of the congregation in various ways, as well as by supportive consultation with the nominating and personnel committee. The pastor plays an even more direct role in "equipping the saints" in the training of members for their service. In fact, this role is so important that we will deal with it in detail in the next chapter. The rest of this chapter will be given to the development of an effective nominating and personnel committee able to maximize the discovery and utilization of potential lay leadership in the church.

Developing a Nominating–Personnel Committee

The following process will result in the development of an ongoing long-range leadership personnel program, maximizing the use of lay persons in the work of the church:

1. Build a functioning nominating-personnel committee
2. Identify *needed* leadership positions
3. Discover potential leaders
4. Select the most qualified persons for specific positions
5. Enlist the leaders selected for service
6. Plan functional training opportunities for all leaders
7. Provide supportive supervision

Following is a brief description of methods and procedures we have found effective for actualizing these components of an effective nominating-personnel committee:

1. Build a Functioning Nominating-Personnel Committee

a. *Purpose.* This committee is responsible for providing the congregation with skilled leadership for carrying out its ministry. Whatever the name, every congregation has, or should have, such a committee.

The first responsibility of this group is to clearly and adequately define its purpose. Too often this committee thinks too small, feeling that its purpose is simply to fill leadership vacancies annually. This committee needs to ask a more inclusive question as to why it exists. Actually, *its purpose is to provide the human resources to lead the congregation in carrying out its ministries in achieving God's mission.* Such a purpose goes much deeper than finding persons to fill jobs annually. It places the responsibility of this group at the heart of facilitating or blocking the church's ability to perform its ministry. Persons are the only means the church has to express and enact the gospel, hence no committee has a more significant role than the nominating-personnel committee when properly conceived.

b. *Composition and Structure.* Members of this committee should have a clear sense of the church's mission, an in-depth perspective of the local congregation, and be well acquainted with church members and their interests as well as their potential talents. A committee of eight or ten members is needed to give the breadth of knowledge of persons and positions as well as to allow for representation of various ages, and diversity of membership needed. The committee needs to have both continuity and new members each year so that a policy of three-year rotating terms will provide three new members each year. The pastor should be a member of this committee because of his or her exposure to all areas of the church life as well as to all the individual members.

c. *Procedures and Work Analysis.* Too frequently this committee meets only once or twice a year to fill vacancies on an annual basis through a quick verbal nomination process. The inadequacy of such procedures is evident by the inactivity of many persons nominated in this way and the large quantity of unused potential leadership in every congregation. A radical change in the operational procedures of most nominating committees is called for.[1]

First of all, the nominating committee needs to view itself as an ongoing, year-round committee to resource all programs and activities with qualified leadership. Its members might begin by becoming familiar with personnel systems for doing job definitions, identifying, enlisting and training personnel. They then might analyze and evaluate the current approach in their local church. They are then ready to develop their own approach to establishing a leadership system.

As the committee members develop a work analysis for their own responsibilities, the following items need attention, along with others they will discover:

1. delineation of policies that will guide their decisions;
2. the determination of the functions and tasks needing to be performed;

3. a leadership study of all church members regarding jobs held, length of service, age, sex, distance from church, and so on;
4. alternative methods of discovering the most qualified persons for each position;
5. a system for recording and cataloging the leadership interests, abilities, and service experience of all members;
6. a long-range leadership development system;
7. plans for going beyond recruitment to training and supportive supervision of leaders;
8. emphasis on the centrality and significance of the leadership role of lay persons in the church.

2. Identify the Needed Leadership Positions

After the nominating personnel committee has identified its own purpose, agreed on its policy guidelines, and set forth the scope and areas of responsibility of its work, it is ready to begin its functional task. Its first job is to clearly identify the functions and tasks of the church's ministry requiring leadership.

a. The committee should examine the stated goals of the congregation and the organizational structures, programs, and activities set up to achieve them. This will indicate where leaders are currently serving. They then need to go beyond this survey to look for possible duplication and lack of coordination. In addition, some goals and their achievement may require that new or additional functions be performed requiring leadership. The committee must be constantly aware that only meaningful and significant tasks will challenge and motivate leaders. Busywork and duplicative tasks may need to be eliminated. This may involve making recommendations to the church administrative board regarding changes in organization. Detailed information needs to be gathered about every area of ministry and service of the subgroups in the church. This includes information about their purpose, goals, methods of operation, activities, number of persons involved, frequency of meetings, and so forth. Before beginning to search for leaders, the nominating and personnel committee must know *where* leadership is needed, *why* leaders are needed, *what* is expected of them, and the *skills* and abilities required. This committee must develop a comprehensive perspective of the mission and ministries of the church for which it is seeking to provide quality leadership.

b. When all leadership positions needed have been agreed upon, the next step is to develop a detailed job description for each one. Hopefully, much of this has been done for incumbent leaders, but existing job descriptions will need to be reexamined and updated. The following items will be useful in developing the various job descriptions:[2]

1. Position or committee.
2. Leadership and committee membership needed.
3. What is the purpose of the group?
4. How does it fit into the purpose and goals of the church?
5. List the tasks the leaders need to perform.
6. What other tasks of other church groups are related to it?
7. What are the duties and skills required of the chairperson?
8. How much time will be required in doing the task well?
   for the chairperson?
   for committee members?
9. Should the present program be expanded?
10. What is the recommended tenure?
    for chairperson?
    for members?
    Why?
11. What resorces and training opportunities are provided?

All job descriptions should be kept in a permanent file and updated regularly.

This kind of careful preparation and data gathering will enable the committee to move into what is traditionally regarded as its main tasks, the discovering and enlisting of leadership for the work of the church.

3. Discover Potential Leaders.

We indicated earlier that one basic underlying concept of leadership development is that every local church has an untapped potential of human resources and talents. The nominating and personnel committee is to discover them, develop them, and utilize them for the work of the church.

The critical question here is, How can the committee become aware of the leadership potential and interests of individual persons in the church? This involves not only unveiling the "hidden" potential in members, but motivating them to active service. This difficult task will require creativity and the use of several approaches.

a. The stewardship of time and talent needs to be emphasized consistently throughout the church. This is a part of each member's faith commitment. The pastor should regularly underscore this concept in preaching, in teaching, in training new members, and in personal conversations. Such theological undergirding will help raise the consciousness of members that their participation in the church's work and ministry is an integral part of the life-style of Christians.

b. A systematic survey of interests and skills of all members needs to be developed; and the information gathered should be cataloged, filed, and kept up to date. Such an instrument will not be sufficient in and of itself, but it is essential to have such information available in written form for the committee. We will discuss other ways of securing data about individuals shortly.

The most helpful talent-indicator instruments are those developed by the nominating personnel committee after developing their job descriptions for all functional tasks of the church. Such a device can be very specific in regard to functional service needs of the local church. Perhaps the following illustration will be helpful to you as you develop your own survey:

1. Include general information, such as, name, address, telephone, date of birth, occupation, hobbies, education.
2. Identify the broad service areas in which leadership and service are needed. For example, one church includes: worship, educational work, evangelism, missions and Christian outreach, community and social concerns, caring and crisis ministries, stewardship and finance, trustees and property, music, administration, clerical, publicity and general.[3]

Each of the above areas should then be broken down into specific skill needs. For instance, the "educational work" heading listed the following skill areas needed:

Teach: nursery, kindergarten, primary, juniors, junior high, senior high, young adults, adults, special short-term courses, assistant teacher, substitute, vacation church/school

Help with special programs and events:
pianist
visitor
telephoner
superintendent of a department; general, indicate age group superintendent
secretarial and clerical help
librarian
youth group counselor or committee, junior, junior high, senior high, older youth
Boy or Girl Scout worker
choir director
camp counselor
operator for audio visual equipment

The breaking down of each general area of service into the actual specific skill and talent needs not only helps individual persons become aware of the many opportunities for service, but also pinpoints precisely where they may be most interested in service.

Persons need the option of indicating various levels of interest, experience, and willingness to serve for each specific item. We suggest therefore that there be five columns after each item to be checked as each person desires. These columns might be headed: (1) some interest, (2) previous experience, (3) currently active, (4) will serve if needed, (5) not now, but future interest.

Once such an instrument is developed, ways must be found to gather the information from all members. There are several options, and each committee will need to make its own decision in the light of their local circumstances. The least effective way is to mail the questionnaire out or distribute it with the church bulletin to be mailed back. Other, more productive methods are: neighborhood house meetings at which the questionnaires are filled out, and followed by calling on absentees; stewardship visitation, with visitors going to each home; interviews during a commitment Lenten visitation; or an act of dedication during a worship service. A creative committee will find other ways to gather the information.

Once the information is gathered, it needs to be cataloged and filed for each person, both by name and by tasks and functions. One final word—the information must be kept up to date, and this requires a talented steward secretary to get the information from new members, to withdraw information regarding members who die or leave the church, and to update information on all members periodically.

c. The information on the talent-and-service instrument needs to be supplemented by the personal knowledge of the members of the committee on nominations and personnel, the pastor, and the current workers in each area. Persons working in one area are frequently aware of others interested in and capable of serving in that area. The pastor(s) usually has many relationships with a large number of church members in varying situations and can share information with the committee relative to otherwise unknown interests and skills of members. When the nominations and personnel committee needs more information about specific persons, it may delegate one of its members to interview the person or persons involved. This kind of personal knowledge and contact can flesh out the written information of questionnaires and be of great help as the committee seeks to enlist the service of members for the work of the church.

4. Select the Most Qualified Persons for Specific Positions

The nominating-personnel committee is now ready to begin matching the leadership needs of the church with specific persons who are best qualified for each position. The importance of this task can hardly be overstated. The quality of leadership is the most important single factor in determining the effectiveness of the achievement of the church's ministry.

Before beginning to suggest names for specific jobs it is well to agree on procedures that will maximize the use of the data gathered and the creativity of the committee. Each nominating committee member should have the job descriptions developed as well as the results of the interest-talent of all church members. It is important at the outset to agree that all evaluations of persons for positions are confidential within the committee. Experience suggests that the usual method of verbal nominations for each leadership position has some serious drawbacks. Such a process gives an advantage to the committee member(s) who think and speak quickly, though not always wisely. Such a verbal nomination process also tends to stifle additional nominations after the first name or two, and to make further nominations seem competitive.

Let us suggest a method that will utilize the creative thinking of all committee members in bringing to the surface the best possible leadership for all positions. Experience indicates it is wise to first nominate all individual church officers and chairpersons of all committees, and then committee members. This ensures placing the most qualified leaders in positions of greatest responsibility. When the committee is ready to make a nomination for a specific position, ask each member to write down the names of the three persons they believe to be best qualified. Collect the cards and list all names on newsprint. This brings out the best thinking of all committee members at once, and discussion can then ensure as each suggested name is evaluated. It gets the best thinking of every member before the entire group and neutralizes the possible control of the committee by the fast-talking, fast-thinking person. The committee members should then select their top three choices, so that if the top choice is unable to serve when approached, they can go immediately to their second or third choice. In addition, the entire list of nominees gives the committee a running start when they later come back to select committee members in that area. This process of selection of persons for specific positions stimulates both creativity and total participation by all committee members. Most important, it facilitates finding the "right" persons for all positions.

5. Enlist the Leaders Selected for Service

After the nominating and personel committee has agreed on leadership candidates, it still remains to secure their consent to serve. How this is done is important because it may affect whether a person accepts and even the quality of performance after acceptance. Enlistment of leaders is really a time of contracting with leaders, of reaching an understanding with them of what the job is they are being asked to do, and specifically what is expected of them as well as the resources and training that will be available.

Sometimes persons find out about their nomination for church jobs through mimeographed lists posted on a bulletin board or mailed out in the church paper. Other committees write personal letters to the nominees. Still other committees use the telephone to inform nominees. *The only effective, responsible contact is a face-to-face visit.* When a person is being asked to give of his or her time to render significant service to the church in carrying out its ministry, a person-to-person conversation is called for. Our experience is that such conversations are most effective if two members of the committee call on each proposed officer or committee chairperson. One committee member and the chairperson then call on other proposed committee members.

Enlistment calls should include at least the following items. The visitors should explain in detail the process used by the committee in arriving at its decision to select the nominee, so the nominee will appreciate the seriousness with which the committee has gone about its task. The visitors will then want to go over the written job description carefully with the nominee, encouraging questions and response. They will also want to work out a clear understanding regarding the expectations regarding what is expected in terms of service, the skills needed, the time required, the tenure of the job, the resources available, and training and support offered. An honest, frank, mutual understanding of expectations will enhance future performance if the responsibility is accepted.

Should the potential leader be undecided but interested, the visitors should offer assistance and suggestions as to how he or she can explore the invitation further by talking with others, perhaps with those currently serving, through observing the functioning of the leader or group, or by getting more informational material for the prospect. In any case, a definite call-back date should be established to finalize a decision.

6. Plan Functional Training Opportunities for All Leaders.

Although most nominating committees do not concern themselves with leadership training, personnel committees must do so, and we have been discussing a nominating-personnel committee. You may need to change your church structure or the functioning of this committee to provide for training of leaders. This commitee does not need to do or even plan the training in detail, but it must be in collaboration with those who do. Leadership enlistment and training must be viewed together as a common endeavor. The next chapter will deal specifically with the training of leaders.

The nominating-personnel committee will want to develop approaches to orient prospective leaders to their new responsibilities. In some cases this may become a part of the decision-making process of acceptance. In other cases it will be a way of getting the new leaders on board to more effectively begin their leadership responsibility. Ways should be found to familiarize potential leaders with the settings in which they will work and how their future groups are now operating. They may want to observe present performance or interview those currently working in the area. A common retreat with "new" and "old" leaders present may sometimes be helpful. Prospective leaders will also want to become familiar with the material resources (books, audiovisual, equipment), budget resources, and skills of other persons in the group.

If training is to meet the needs of leaders and group members, a process needs to be developed to let them express their training needs as they assess themselves in relation to the job description and in conversation with those now working in that area. Training must be focused on the needs of persons in leadership positions. This concept will be expanded in the next chapter. If potential leaders are aware that helpful training will be available to them, it will encourage their acceptance and enhance their performance.

7. Provide Supportive Supervision

It is not enough simply to enlist persons for church leadership positions. A church should celebrate the acceptance of leadership responsibilities by lay persons in a public commissioning or consecration service during the worship hour.

Leaders need continuous support as they function in their specific areas. The pastor can express an encouraging and supportive word from time to time, or share periods of struggle and working through difficulties. It is also important to provide supportive groups of co-laborers and leaders where new and experienced colleagues can share openly with one another. No church leader should experience a sense of isolation. A very specific expression of support is evident when the church provides adequate resources for the task on all levels, including the needed persons with whom to work.

Leaders need, and most want, to assess how they are doing. A performance analysis structure should be set up to examine how leaders and groups are doing. Ongoing feedback should be sought within each group or committee as well as from all persons affected by the programs or activities of their group.

Increased effectiveness requires that each leader and group relate what is actually happening to the desired outcomes as expressed in the goals of the church. It must never be forgotten that it is the church's ministry to express God's mission, and all service is to be seen in that light.

Chapter 8

Leadership Training

When it comes to discovering and motivating volunteer workers in a church, recruitment and training are essential twins-in-the-process. Yet, in most churches recruitment is done poorly, and training is practically nonexistent. The fact remains, however, that training is the key to releasing the potential for ministry that is resident in the congregation. Good recruitment identifies workers. Training empowers them to be effective in the job they have accepted responsibility to do.

Every person who takes a job in the church becomes a candidate for training. Every program responsibility or role that is filled by someone is a possible area of needed training. If a program responsibility or position requires no training, it can only mean one of two things:

1. The person recruited to fill it has had prior successful training in this area; or
2. The role is of such minor consequence and importance it makes no difference whether it is carried out effectively or not.

If the latter is true, then of course it is dehumanizing to ask any person to fill the role, and it should be abolished forthwith. If, however, the role is important, the leaders of the church are morally obligated to provide sufficient training to ensure the person who is recruited will be able to do an effective and personally rewarding job. If you don't have time to provide training for any job in the church, and a previously trained, competent person cannot be recruited, that position, no matter how important, should not be filled. It should remain vacant until time is available to design and conduct the training.

The reason for or insistance upon training is inherent in contemporary theology, wich is placing more emphasis on the whole people of God, the Body of Christ, lay and clergy, to be corporately involved in ministry. Such theology calls for a more active, educated, reflective laity. Clergy are by no means the only ministers. Laity, too, have a ministry and an obligation to carry it out in the most effective manner possible.

Modern bureaucratic, impersonal society also creates certain imperatives for lay training in the church. Many of the persons who volunteer their services in the church also work in organizations and relate to institutions in which power and status are reserved for a few at the top. A vast majority of persons in such systems are experiencing varying degrees of loneliness, loss of self-esteem, failure—on the job, in school, at home. The church must guard against this in its own programs. Every worker, whether an acolyte, mimeograph operator, or lay leader, must be given all necessary training and resources to assure him opportunity to experience the growth and the thrill of a job well done.

Much of the training the church provides its workers can equip them to experience greater success in their relationships with other organizations. When a Sunday school teacher is trained in interpersonal communications, he or she is learning a set of skills that will improve the quality of his or her relationships at home and at work. When a board member is trained in problem-solving and planning, he or she is learning skills which can be used in business, on the school board and other places. Training is one important ministry to persons and systems that is almost completely ignored by the church.

Training for Effectiveness

Training is always best done when it is a direct reponse to specific goals and programs, and is designed to enable individuals and groups to be more effective in carrying out specific responsibilities in achieving the goals and carrying out the programs. Training must be directly related to what persons do, enabling them to do their jobs more effectively. Without clear goals and program responsibilities to which the persons being trained are vitally committed, training will be ill received, will effect little or no change in a person's behavior, and will produce few lasting benefits for the church. Robert Worley speaks to this when he says:

Activation of members depends upon training designed to equip persons to do those tasks they are committed to do, training which will enable members to be increasingly effective in the limited time available. Training, therefore, depends upon planning, upon enabling persons to do what they have planned. Planning identifies tasks, the order in which tasks need to be performed, and the resources needed to do the task. Training brings the critical elements of a plan together. Tasks, methods of doing the task and resources are brought together in a good training design.

An effective training design used in working with congregations, therefore, has the following elements:

1. *A clear definition of what the* (church officers, committee or task group) *is to do to achieve their objectives.* Tasks should be defined as clearly as possible. Persons who are performing the tasks should see the relation of their tasks to the objective and to the goal which that objective is helping to achieve. Members need to see how what they are doing fits into the whole of congregational life, and that their activity is worthwhile.

2. *The identification of resources needed to do the task.* Resources include ideas, skills, tools, programs, curricula, methods, persons, facilities, and money. Persons may have clarity of task without knowing what resources they will need to acomplish the task. Identifying and gathering resources is part of doing the task. One aspect of resource identification is choosing among alternative resources, which may mean that the committee or task group must develop criteria for selection of resources.

Example. The objective is to identify a curriculum for senior highs, teach curriculum for the fall quarter 1979, and evaluate the class by March 1988. A task in achieving this objective is the selection of one curriculum from numerous curricular resources which exist for this age group. These resources need to be examined and one (or a combination of several) selected. What criteria are to be used in examining and selecting the curriculum?

A training session may be needed for the selecting group to develop a list of criteria they want to use in examining various curricula and making a final selection. First the task group will need to identify what the congregation desires to share of its understanding of Christian faith, and how it desires to share it. The group would then attempt to identify areas of Christian faith and life which their youth are seeking to understand and experience from the congregation, and the forms and style of sharing which would be most helpful.

From its lists of areas of Christian faith most important to the congregation and areas most important to young people, the task group could determine the format and style of resources most appropriate to their particular group of young persons. The task group has a basis then for examining the large variety of resources available and for deciding on the best one for the church's youth.

A plan to schedule tasks and secure resources as needed to achieve the objective. Groups may know what the objective is, understand the tasks needed to achieve the objective, and have resources, but not know how to systematically put objective, tasks, and resources together. Developing a real plan as an important aspect of training increases the possibility that committees and task groups will be effective. A plan indicates next steps to be taken, which increases the prospects that they will be taken. Most training programs inspire, but do not leave groups with concrete ways to proceed when the training is concluded.[1]

Training that is done in the context of specific goals and is designed to enable persons to be more effective is often not recognized as training at all, but as working sessions enabling persons to excel in their areas of interest. The importance of this for motivating persons can hardly be overemphasized.

One of the authors was privileged to serve as a project director in the Chicago Parish Development project. In a report on that project the authors' state:

Training laity to be effective in their tasks involves identifying knowledge, tools,and skills needed, then designing training to actually work on the tasks while developing these knowledge, tools and skills. . . .

An important assumption behind the project was that after years of listening to sermons, participating in the liturgy, and attending adult education classes, the project staff did not have to provide a "correct" theology or purify the theological perspective which members already had. Rather, it was our task to assist lay persons to identify their commitments and their intentions to act on the basis of those commitments. We were not willing to assume that their years of participation in the church meant nothing for the shaping of their faith or that we needed to reshape it. We desired, in the processes we designed, to help them identify those commitments in terms of goals and objectives for the congregation, and to look briefly at what those goals and objectives meant in terms of the quality of their faith. Next we desired to assist them in becoming effective in achieving the goals and objectives which their faith commitments said were important to them.

In working with councils, committees and task groups the goal was to train persons to be effective. The assumption was that effectiveness increases faith commitment, allows persons to act out their commitments more fully, and increases the desire to be more involved in the ministry and mission of the congregation.[2]

Training Needs Inventory

It is helpful to conduct a training needs inventory immediately following a goal-setting process and/or after the annual nominations and election of church leaders. On the following page is a process we have found helpful in conducting the inventory.

Training for Pastors

In most cases the type of lay training we are talking about will have to be initiated by the pastor or it will not be done at all. The pastor need not necessarily do the training, but he or she must envision its need, be able to prepare instructional objectives,[3] and understand something about training design methodologies. This means many pastors themselves need training and skill development to lead the way in supporting and organizing effective training. An unsupportive, uninvolved pastor will almost certainly create a climate in

TRAINING NEEDS INVENTORY

I.   List all of the organization's administrative and program units/positions.
II. Conduct an audit to supply all of the information called for on the chart below.
III. Construct a chart similar to the one below to display the congregation's training needs.

Name of Unit of Position	Goals and Responsibilities. What is it supposed to do?	★1 Tools Needed to do the job well?	★2 Present skill Level of group/ individual	★3 Training needed to increase effectiveness	★4 How Can training be best accomplished? When?

★1   What tools, knowledge, skills are needed to accomplish the goals/responsibilities?
★2   Which of these does the group/individual already possess?
★3   What new tools, knowledge, skills does the group/individual need to be given to do the job effectively?
★4   How can this training best be accomplished? When? (In planning this step be sure to look for similarities of groups' training needs in which case, training of several groups may be provided in the same training event.)

which effective training will not happen. Conversely, a supportive, involved pastor can almost certainly inspire laity to receive training. The ability to be supportive of effective lay training is directly related to one's own self-image and skill level.

Pastors with a low self-image and skill level generally will experience high control needs. One means of maintaining control is to keep the laity perpetually ineffective and therefore dependent upon the pastor.[4]

Providing comprehensive training within a congregation will require a level of effort many pastors are not accustomed to giving. However, few other efforts will achieve such high payoffs in terms of empowering lay persons for effective ministry and program effectiveness.

Conclusion

Effective training actually begins with the recruiting process. When persons are recruited to fill positions, they should be informed of the goals and responsibilities of that position, and that adequate training will be provided to ensure their effectiveness. This goes a long way toward creating a norm throughout the entire organization that effectiveness and training are expected of all who serve.

Training can be provided in many ways. A valuable resource for envisioning various training methods is the little book, *The Volunteer Community*.[5] Every pastor serious about training should benefit from studying its contents.

Earlier in this volume we discussed the need for meaningful reward systems to sustain worker commitment. We return briefly to that subject. Training designed to empower laity to be more effective in achieving goals and interests important to them can be a rewarding experience for all. All persons want to experience success and to be recognized for it. Training and consistent feedback regarding one's level of effectiveness and ministry on behalf of the congregation, indicate that the person and the job are important, that the person is part of a team, and that the leaders notice and care.

Chapter 9
Creating a Supportive Climate

Up to this point, we have explored in detail eight specific ways of empowering lay persons for the church's ministry. In this final chapter, we suggest that the full message and impact of this book is actually more than the sum of its parts. We have discussed how each of the following emphases contributes toward empowering lay persons:

1. Giving priority to spiritual formation
2. Releasing human resources
3. Developing appropriate leadership styles
4. Making effective decisions
5. Assessing the congregation
6. Planning for action
7. Securing responsible leaders
8. Providing useful leadership training

We are now suggesting that *together* these areas of action form a "gestalt," or wholeness, contributing to a supportive climate in the life of the congregation. When all these factors are properly emphasized, the moral of the congregation is lifted, members feel they belong to a caring fellowship, and they are enthusiastic about becoming involved in one or more areas of the church's life as a satisfying way to express their Christian faith.

The subjects discussed in the preceding chapters,

when properly orchestrated, will go a long way toward creating a climate of openness, productivity, and mutual support. Although each of the subjects is important in itself, these concerns together form a sort of collage that appropriates differences of opinion and diversities of interest, bringing them together to enlist a wide variety of skills and commitments.

One prime concern of local churches today is how to deal with differences between members as to what should or should not be going on in the life of the church. This question often results in a conflicting, rather than supportive, climate. Sharp divergences are splitting some congregations apart and are leading to power struggles for control of the church. The need for a supportive climate is evident on every hand, but in many churches the focus of energy is on settling each conflict through some form of power struggle.

A supportive climate is not likely to come out of a power struggle over specific issues. There are times when such existing struggles may need to be dealt with through conflict management processes, but at best that can only clear the way for developing a supportive climate. Through such a climate, divergences and differences can be acknowledged and then used in developing broad and varying ministries of the congregation. A supportive climate calls for a long-term effort to develop the processes and procedures discussed in this volume. It cannot sprout up overnight at the end of a conflict. These processes, over a period of time, will enable a congregation to give primary emphasis to spiritual growth, trust, and involvment in assessing their own needs. These experiences will enable members to determine where they need to focus their energy to effectively make decisions about action plans. The procedure discussed here will challenge leaders and members to discover how to use their diverse skills and interests in carrying out a variety of needed ministries. As clergy and laity share in this participative process, a strengthened supportive climate will emerge.

Defining a Supportive Climate

Before going any further, let us examine the critical question, How would you recognize a supportive climate in a church if you saw one? For some, the answer might be quite simple: It would be a church I would feel good about. Although that might be true, certainly a supportive climate cannot be equated with making every member "feel good." A supportive climate has many dimensions, and we will identify them now to clarify what we are talking about as we use the term in this chapter.

Broadly speaking, the three primary components of a supportive climate are: (1) purpose, (2) persons, and (3) processes.

1) An organization cannot be supportive of either itself or its members unless there is clarity about its *purpose*, its reason for being. Leaders and members must be clear about why the organization exists in order to work and plan together to reach their goal.

2) A mutual concern for persons (fellow members) in the organization is the "raw material" from which a supportive climate is formed. It emerges only as trust develops and persons relate to one another in mutual service and support to achieve their common purpose.

3) The final component of a supportive climate is the use of processes and procedures that facilitate and maximize all human resources in deciding, planning, and carrying out the activities and experiences required to achieve the organization's purpose.

Perhaps the nature of a supportive climate will become clearer as we outline some specific components that are characteristic of a church where a supportive climate exists. This listing will then be followed by an instrument for assessing the supportive climate of your church.

Components of a Supportive Climate in an Organization

A. Purpose

1. *A Clear and Commonly Understood Purpose.* A clear purpose is evidenced by a common commitment, cohesive programs, and clear priorities as guidelines for decision making. Unless the leaders and members of an organization have a common and clear understanding of why they exist and what they are trying to do, confusion and divisiveness will reign. This will be expressed through several factions fighting with one another for control or by a smorgasbord of unrelated activities moving out in all directions, some even competitive with one another.

2. *Sensitivity and Adaptability to Changing Needs.* As situations change, new ways of expressing purpose are required. Openness and sensitivity to needs of persons and groups are basic to a supportive climate. As needs change, so must programs and activities. Adaptability keeps an organization current and elicits continuing support from persons and groups whose needs are being met.

3. *Diversity of Programs Linked to Purpose.* A sense of purpose in an organization keeps it from developing a smorgasbord of unrelated programs without any cohesion. Diverse programs require the connecting link of purpose if any sense of mutuality or team identification is to exist. A sense of identity with other co-workers, even in diverse programs, is basic to a supportive organizational climate.

B. Persons

4. *Compatibility of Personal and Organizational Goals.* When individuals perceive that their personal needs are being met through their involvement and service to the church, they experience a sense of fulfillment. When this happens, loyalty and productivity of organizational goals will increase because persons are finding their

church involvement challenging, growth producing, and exciting. Such experiences contribute much to building a supportive climate in a church.

5. *Mutual Concern of Persons for One Another* (Lay and Clergy). A genuine concern for the worth and well-being of persons must be top priority in any church. Each person needs to feel important, wanted, needed, a part of a caring fellowship. This will come about when members' needs are served and when they become participants in work, service, study or interest groups of their choice and they really feel accepted and at home.

6. *Maximum Use of Leader and Member Resources.* As members are welcomed to share leadership with clergy, the development of mutual trust contributes to a supportive climate. Members are encouraged, supported, and trained to carry out their leadership responsibilities. They all have a sense of belonging to a team of workers sharing a common task.

7. *Acceptance of Minority Views and Persons.* Not everyone agrees on issues in an organization. Minority views need to be listened to carefully and not simply put down. Most important, persons holding minority views must be respected. Minority groups and persons are a part of an organization, and their voices in decision-making and planning bodies are basic. Any plans made must take into account minority needs, positions, and feelings.

C. *Processes*

8. *Clear and Open Communication Channels.* Clear communication requires careful listening as well as clear expression of a point of view. Feelings, as well as content, need to be both expressed and "heard." Openness and honesty in communication are required if sound decisions are to result. Proper communication channels must be established so that everyone knows whom to talk to about what. Openness in dealing with conflict is essential, though painful.

9. *Decisions Made by the Affected Groups.* Nothing can make the development of a supportive organizational

climate more difficult than "vest pocket" decisions made by a few behind closed doors. If a supportive climate has anything to do with having a sense of belonging, ownership, and commitment to an organization, then persons and groups affected by decisions must be involved in making them.

10. *Reality Testing.* Every organization needs to know how it is doing. If it is not meeting real needs, sooner or later it will find out, perhaps by having to close down. Reliable feedback evaluation is essential and depends upon an honest, open response by those within and without the organization. An open assessment of a church by its members and the community provides necessary data for future planning and gives specific clues as to how to develop a more supportive climate.

The above items make up the main components of a supportive climate in an organization, particularly the church. Some of these items can be dealt with head on. Others are "by-products" of a number of experiences and programs found in the ongoing life of the church. We believe that the approaches detailed in the eight previous chapters will have a very significant impact on all ten of these components.

You may be interested in assessing the supportive climate of your church. If so, you may want to fill in the instrument on pages 127-128, which we have designed for this purpose. It will be most helpful if each person will fill it in individually without talking with others. Individual perceptions should then be shared with others as a basis of discussion, to determine what is needed to improve your situation.

Establishing a Supportive Climate

Establishing a supportive climate in your church is a joint responsivility of clergy and lay persons. The beginning point is the development of teamwork between the clergy and lay persons in leadership positions in the church.

CONTINUUM FOR ASSESSING
THE SUPPORTIVE CLIMATE OF A CHURCH

A. *PURPOSE*

1. Clear and commonly understood purpose

Uncertainty and confusion about purpose	1 2 3 4 5	Members are clear about the purpose of the church

2. Sensitivity and Adaptability to changing needs

Change is resisted and comes slowly	1 2 3 4 5	Sensitive and adaptable to changes related to purpose

3. Diversity of programs but each linked to purpose

Traditional programs and they are independent, lacking cohesion	1 2 3 4 5	Diverse programs to meet many needs, each expressive of church's purpose

B. *PERSONS*

4. Compatibility of personal and organizational goals

People pushed into jobs with little concern for what happens to them	1 2 3 4 5	Persons choose to become involved in tasks that are fulfilling for them

5. Mutual concern of persons for one another

Members feel alone, isolated, indifferent	1 2 3 4 5	Members have a sense of "belonging" to a caring fellowship

6. Maximum use of leader-member resources

A few people do the work of the church	1 2 3 4 5	Leadership and jobs are shared by many

7. Acceptance of minority views and persons

Minority views and persons are ignored	1 2 3 4 5	Minority views and persons respected, and plans made accordingly

C. PROCESS

8. Clear and open communication channels

Little listening, confused communication	1	2	3	4	5	Open communication, people know who to talk to about what

9. Decisions are made by the affected groups

Decisions made by a few behind closed doors	1	2	3	4	5	Groups affected are involved in making decisions

10. Reality testing

No feedback from members and non-members	1	2	3	4	5	Formal and informal feedback from members and non-members

The pastor needs to lead out in demonstrating a sense of trust and integrity toward the lay leadership, as well as confidence in their ability. The key to building a supportive climate rests on establishing a working, trusting relationship between pastor and lay leadership which will filter through to a similar relationship between the lay leadership and the membership at large, and through them to nonmembers with whom the church comes in contact. Organizational research clearly establishes the fact that the leadership style and attitudes determine the response and behavior of the membership.

This means that the pastor must sincerely desire to have an active laity, must cease operating in a "Lone Ranger" style, and must give wholehearted attention to working *with* and *through* the people to do the ministry of the church. Thomas Jefferson said:

Leaders by their constitutions are naturally divided into two parties: those who fear and distrust the people and wish to draw all powers from them for their own benefit, and those who identify with the people, have confidence in them, and cherish and consider them as honest and safe with public interest.

128

The degree of power felt by the laity within any church is greatly influenced by the pastor's view of the congregation's ability to handle power, make decisions, and choose worthy goals. The same principle operates in the way those lay persons function who are chairpersons of committees and boards, in relation to how they work with other members. The tone of a supportive climate, or lack of it, is set by the leadership. This is expressed in the manner by which goals and purpose are determined, the degree of trust and caring experienced in interpersonal relationships, and the participative and supportive teamwork evident in the organizational process used in carrying out the work of the church.

Supportive leadership will draw persons to committed service to the church, because such leaders believe that the people are capable and creative in solving problems and making decisions. They will view failure not as sin but as part of the growing process. They will tend to set persons free to explore ministries in keeping with their own interests, and will lead the congregation in celebrating every small and great success. This type of leadership throws open the windows to the spirit of God, empowering both clergy and laity.

Perhaps you want to give persons a larger role in planning and doing ministry, but you are not sure they want it or that they can actually do it. These words of Goethe, then, are for you: "Treat people as if they are what they ought to be, and you help them become what they are capable of becoming."

It is our hope that God will have spoken to you through your reading of this book to "let my people go, that they may serve me." Our aim has been to suggest explicit ways of freeing the lay potential of the church to be engaged more effectively in the church's ministry of expressing God's mission today.

Notes

Chapter 1. Spiritual Formation

1. From the *Ledger*, Lakeland, Florida, February 25, 1978.
2. New York Times, February 24, 1978.
3. Alvin J. Lindgren, *Foundations for Purposeful Church Administration* (Nashville: Abingdon Press, 1965), pp. 43-52.

Chapter 2: Releasing Human Resources

1. The concept of "stroking" was started by Eric Berne, founder of transactional analysis. Dr. Berne had a quip that went something like this: "If a puppy isn't stroked every day, its spine will shrivel." Research has shown people can become sick and die in the absence of meaningful strokes—rewards that inform them of their self-worth and importance to others. This may be a primary reason that many persons become senile or die soon after retirement from their jobs.
2. We are aware that various segments of the church growth movement are emphasizing homogeneity of theology and programs in the local church as a means of spurring membership growth. We are of the opinion, however, that merely attracting members, many of whom will be passive, having no opportunity for meaningful volunteer service due to narrowness of programs, is hardly a sufficient criterion for evaluating true growth in the church. We are not opposed to increased numbers—far from it. What we are here advocating is a breadth of service opportunities sufficient to utilize the interests and skills of all the members without asking them to sacrifice their own understanding of Christian service to that of another.
3. Presbyterian Book of Order, United Methodist Book of Discipline, Catholic Cannon Law, and others.

Chapter 3. Appropriate Leadership Style

1. Rensis Likert, New Patterns of Management (New York: McGraw-Hill, 1961).
2. James V. Spotts, "The Problem of Leadership" in Behavioral Science and the Manager's Role, William Eddy, et al., eds. (Arlington, Va.: National Training Laboratories, 1969).
3. Reprinted by permission of the Harvard Business Review. Exhibit from "How to Choose a Leadership Pattern" by Robert Tannenbaum and Warren H. Schmidt (May-June 1973). Copyright © 1973 by the President and Fellows of Harvard College; all rights reserved.
4. Robert Blake and Jane Mouton, Building a Dynamic Corporation Through Grid Organization Development, © 1969, Addison-Wesley Publishing Company, Inc., Reading, Mass. Adaptation from pages 60-62. Reprinted with permission.
5. The Managerial Grid figure from The Managerial Grid by Robert R. Blake and Jane Srygley Mouton. Copyright © 1978. (Houston: Gulf Publishing Company), p. 11. Reproduced by permission.
6. For detailed research and a full description of the interactionist approach to leadership, see James V. Spotts, Kansas Business Review, June 1964. pp. 3-13.
7. Fred E. Fiedler, "Style or Circumstance: The Leadership Enigma," in Psychology Today, March 1969.
8. You may discover your own present leadership styles and your ability to match them to the needs of the group by use of a survey instrument, Taking a Look at Your Leadership Styles, Norman Shawchuck (Downers Grove, Ill. Organization Resources Press, 1977).
9. "The Center Letter," Center for Parish Development, Naperville, Ill., October 1974.

Chapter 4. Effective Decision Making

1. Edgar Schein, Process Consultation: Its Role in Organization Development (Reading, Mass. Addison-Wesley, 1969).
2. Richard Schmuck and Philip Runkel, Handbook of Organization Development in Schools (Palo Alto: National Press Books, 1972; 2nd. ed. 1977, Mayfield Publishing Co.).
3. Ibid.

Chapter 5. Congregational Assessment

1. Two recommended resources dealing with assessment, and other public change processes, are: Robert Worley, Dry Bones Breathe (Chicago: Center for the Study of Church Organiza-

tional Behavior, 1978); and H. Rhea Gray, G. Douglass Lewis, Norman Shawchuck, Robert Worley, *Experiences in Activating Congregations,* (Chicago: The Institute for Ministry Development, 1978).

2. A good rule of thumb to use when considering the use of questionnaires in assessment is, "an assessment questionnaire is worth only as much as the discussion it generates among the members of the group." Assessment questionnaires without discussion generate little ownership or action on the part of the group. Use questionnaires without group discussion only as a last resort.

3. Sometimes members within the congregation will use the assessment process as a means of griping and complaining about the pastor, programs, ecclesiastical officials. We say they are "dumping their garbage." If the pastor and workers do not become defensive, and at the same time do not allow a negative person to completely dominate the process, a few persons dumping garbage will have no negative effect upon the assessment.

4. It is not necessary that the pastor or lay officials attend all the home meetings, since the information from all of them will be finally brought together into one report. A group of fourteen should perhaps be subdivided into two groups of seven, each meeting in different rooms in the home and each having a trained leader.

5. It is vital that the home meeting leaders be fully trained and equipped to conduct the home meetings and to record the assessment information that is generated. See Appendix A, a sample training piece that each leader can also use when actually conducting the meeting. It is good to actually take the leaders through a complete home meeting process to allow them the actual experience of it.

6. See Appendix B for a flow chart showing the possible steps in an assessment utilizing home meetings.

7. The steps listed within number 3 are described in detail in an excellent book. *Management and Organization Development,* by Christ Argyris (New York: McGraw-Hill, 1971.)

Chapter 6. Planning for Action

1. For a full treatment of results of an organization caught in the activity trap, see George Odiorne, *Management and the Activity Trap,* (New York: Harper & Row, 1974).

2. Alvin J. Lindgren and Norman Shawchuck, *Management for Your Church* (Nashville: Abingdon, 1977).

3. In addition to our earlier volume, *Management for Your*

Church, there are two other resources we recommend for goal setting/planning. They are *Dry Bones Breathe*, Robert Worley; and *Congregational Goals Discovery Plan* (Newton, Kn: Faith and Life Press, 1976).

4. The following evaluation questions, along with helps for planning and doing the evaluation is given in *Fundamentals of Evaluation*, Norman Rath, Shawchuck, Stoyanoff (Downers Grove, Ill.: Organization Resources Press, 1979).

5. Denominational planners are aware of the growing inability of the old structures to satisfy the needs of today's church, and as a result have initiated new structures, such as the Council on Ministries of The United Methodist Church and the new Synod arrangements of The United Presbyterian Church in the U.S.A. In some instances, however, these new structures are meeting with increasing opposition. Satisfactory organizational structures cannot be created for a local church without first identifying the unique needs of the church and its immediate environment. Opposition is raised to new structures when they are imposed upon the local church in an attempt to make it reflect the denomination's structures.

Pressure to model every church alike determines the character of the denomination and its churches. Such pressure stifles creativity and causes the local church to be inflexible and insensitive to a rapidly changing environment. The most effective church structures will be determined not by ecclesiastical polity but by the unique theological values and missional priorities of each congregation as it tries to be the Body of Christ in its immediate environment and in the world (see Appendix B).

In our opinion, the need for sufficient uniformity of structures to maintain the denomination's identity and programs, and the need for sufficient flexibility to assure commitment to and achievement of local goals are not irreconcilable. Both needs can be met. Local and denominational leaders must operate in the necessary tension between the two important needs. The ultimate test of effectiveness, however, is not whether the structures satisfy denominational legislation, but whether they enable the resources of the local church to assure maximal realization of its goals and plans. A beginning move in this direction was made when *The Book of Discipline of the United Methodist Church* offered an option to local churches to design their own structure, with the approval of the district superintendent.

Where size, circumstances, and specific mission responsibilities demand, a local church may in consultation with and approval by the district superintendent modify the organizational plans hereinafter set forth; *provided* that adequate provisions shall be made in such an organizational plan for relating the local church structures to appropriate district, Annual Conference, jurisdictional, and general church agencies and structures. (The Book of Discipline 1976, The United Methodist Church, par. 262.)

6. Thomas Gordon, *Leader Effectiveness Training* (Wyden Books, 1977), pp. 244-45.
7. Adapted from *Developing Attitudes Toward Learning* by Robert F. Mager, copyright © 1968 by Fearon Publishers, Inc.; reprinted by permission of Pitman Learning, Inc., Belmont, California.

Chapter 7. Securing Responsible Leaders

1. For a more detailed discussion of the functioning of a nominating-personnel committee, see Alvin J. Lindgren, *Foundations of Purposeful Church Administration*, Chap. 8, pp. 181-225.
2. Adapted from ibid, pp. 202-3.
3. Ibid.

Chapter 8. Leadership Training

1. Robert C. Worley, *Dry Bones Breathe*, pp. 95-96. Quoted with permission of author.
2. Gary, Lewis, Shawchuck, Worley, *Experiences in Activating Congregations*, pp.98 and 77-78.
3. A most helpful reference is Robert Mager's *Preparing Instructional Objectives* (Belmont, Cal.: Fearon Press, 1975).
4. The Parish Development Project speaks to this in Ibid.: "Pastors who had high control needs . . . did not desire activation, except on their terms. Several pastors were actually fearful of congregations and processes which might activate members for ministry and mission" (p. 106).
5. Eva Schindler-Rainman and Ronald Lippitt, *The Volunteer Community* (Arlington, VA.: National Training Laboratories, 1975).

Appendix A

Congregational Assessment

Home Meeting Leaders Training Design
and
Format for the Home Meeting

MATERIALS: Name tags, pens, information cards, questionnaires, envelopes. Optional: coffee, large paper
and markers.

PURPOSE: To lead the group through a discussion of our
church; its strengths, weaknesses, hopes and
opportunities for ministry.

Actual Meeting

(Meet and greet each person as he arrives. Ask each person to wear
a name tag. As people are assembling, you can ask them to fill out
the information card, which is an attempt to update the mailing
list—one card per family.)

Introduction (5 Minutes)

(*Begin by briefly explaining why you have gathered.*)
As you know from the pulpit announcements and from the
phone calls to all the members, we have come together this
evening to share our feelings and thoughts about our church. All
members are being asked to contribute their ideas and feelings
about our church so that all of us together can make our church
the kind of community that will help each of us to deepen, to
express, and to share our belief in Christ with one another.

Background

We have been able to gather tonight because some of our fellow
members have been working to plan just how the whole

135

membership could most effectively be reached so that each person could contribute his or her feelings and ideas about our church. From time to time we have all read about the progress of this group in the newsletter. A couple of weeks ago we (*you might mention your names*) volunteered to act as Process Assistants and Home Greeters. We were given a list of people in this area to contact and to invite to a meeting such as this. The purpose of our meeting tonight is to explore together how each of us sees our church and to ask ourselves what each of us would like to see our church become!

Approach

The way in which we would like to go about this task is to discuss a few questions. These are the same questions being discussed in all the home meetings. The results of all these discussions will be made available to all the members. We hope the home meetings will provide a good picture of what we want our church to be. Once we have this picture, we can all begin working to make our church the kind of community that will assist each member to deepen, to express, and to share his or her belief in Christ with others in the church and in the community at large. (*Possibly allow for questions regarding "why we have gathered" at this time.*)

Discussion (5 Minutes)

Tonight, each of us is here because each of us, in our own way, values our affiliation with our church. It is important for us to share our views about our church with one another so that, together, we can construct the kind of fellowship that will be of service to all of us.

Round I (40 minutes)

What we would like to do now is to ask you to focus on two questions:
1. What are the strengths of our church? What is going for us?
2. What are the weaknesses and/or major problems of our church? What is going against us?

We are allowing forty minutes for the discussion. Perhaps we should break up into groups of six or seven for the discussion.

Note:Make sure each group understands the questions. Have them written in large letters for display in each group.

We ask one person in each group to play "participant-recorder" by taking down the ideas and feelings expressed so that we can get back together at the end of the forty minutes to hear our perceptions. If you are recording, don't forget to voice your own views too!

Appendix A

Note: 1. Groups should be in separate rooms if possible.
2. Groups should be given large pieces of paper upon which to make public their views—this would also help in the sharing session later.
3. The leader should participate in the discussion but not act as recorder.
4. After forty minutes, gather the groups together and have each report their findings.

Total Group (20 Minutes)

Now we will hear a brief report from each group regarding their response to the questions. *(Allow brief questions for clarification following each report, but do not allow argument of opinion.)*

Round II (40 minutes)

I think that we can appreciate the diversity of opinions as well as the areas upon which we have seen general agreement. Having taken a look at our church as it has been for us, let us take another forty minutes to discuss two more questions:
1. What are your hopes and dreams for our church for the next one to five years?
2. What specific suggestions do you have for ministering to our community, near and afar?

(Possibly this time, someone else in the group could act as recorder. Follow the suggestions given above.)

Total Group (30 Minutes)

Once again we will hear a brief report from each group. (After the reports, say———.)

Conclusion

We have all spent some time this evening discussing our mutual hopes and concerns for our church!

As you heard the reports, what points of similarity did you hear? What were the most striking differences? List the similarities and differences.

As we mentioned earlier, the survey results will be tabulated in the next couple of weeks and will be made available for all parishioners.

(If your church is also using the home-meeting format for reporting to the congregation, say:)

What we would like to do is to invite all of you back here when the results are available so that we can pool our ideas about what we can do to make our church the kind of parish we want.

(If possible, set an exact date and time for the next meeting, elicit

137

the help of a few in setting up the meeting—refreshments, place, etc.)

The group leaders may want to ask those present how they feel about the meeting they just completed—e.g., Was it helpful or profitable? Do they feel positive or negative about it?)

Thanks for coming, and we hope to see all of you at our next meeting!

(Dismiss with prayer for success of assessment process.)

Leader's Report

The leaders should prepare a summary of the meeting—ideas expressed in discussion, especially trends that emerged, people's reaction to the meeting, the date and place and time established for the next meeting, as well as a personal word of evaluation for use in preparing the compiled assessment reports.

Appendix B

FLOWCHART: ASSESSMENT PROCESS FOR A LOCAL CHURCH

WHO	DOES WHAT	WHEN	WHY ARE WE DOING THIS?	EXPECTED RESULTS
Pastor	Introduce assessment process to administrative board, outline benefits, answers, questions, etc.	Aug. 3 Board meeting	It is essential for the board to understand the process before they can make informed decisions about it.	Board approval
Administrative Board	Pass resolution calling for the assessment process and recruit an assessment steering committee.	Aug. 3-15	It is necessary for the administrative board to "own" the process as their own, and to provide for lay leadership.	Assessment process legitimized and lay steering committee recruited.
Administrative Board	Announce assessment plans to entire congregation; introduce steering committee and answer questions.	Sept. 1 & 8:	The congregation must be aware of the process and its benefits before they can be expected to support it and participate.	The first step toward getting congregational ownership and participation.
Pastor and Steering Committee	Plan assessment process to include home meetings (one for every 14 members), and a "statistical information team."	Sept. 2,9, & 16: Three weekly meeting.	To plan each step of the process in order to schedule events and determine volunteer workers and resource needs.	An action plan for the assessment process.
Steering Committee	Introduce plan to the congregation, announce number of volunteer workers needed, and what they will do. Recruit leaders for home meetings, and the statistical information team.	Sept. 22 & 29: Worship services and personal contacts.	To assure participation we must keep people informed. Members will only volunteer when they support the program and know what they will be expected to do.	An informed congregation, growing interest in the assessment. Volunteer workers recruited.

All of the dates given on the flowchart are to be taken as suggestive only. It may take much less or more time to do a similar process in your church.

WHO	DOES WHAT	WHEN	WHY ARE WE DOING THIS?	EXPECTED RESULTS
Pastor	Train leaders and the steering committee to invite persons to home meetings, conduct meetings and collate the information.	Oct. 6: Afternoon and evening sessions.	Every worker needs to be trained to carry out his/her function in the process.	Trained, able workers, each with resources needed to do his/her job.
Sociologist, professor, etc.	Train statistical information team to gather and chart the information.	Same as above.	Same as above.	Same as above.
Steering Committee, Home Leaders & Statistical Information Team	Potluck dinner and inspirational prayer service for success of assessment program.	Oct. 6: 5:30–7:00 P.M.	To build inspiration among workers and to emphasize the sacredness of the program.	Better acquainted, highly motivated workers
Steering Committee and Home Leaders	Assign persons to be invited to home meetings—no more than 14 per home. Set dates for home meetings.	Oct. 10: Evening.	So each leader can be involved in deciding who will attend their home meeting. To be sure that every person in congregation is personally invited to attend a home meeting.	Leaders given a list of persons who are to be invited to their home meeting.
Steering Committee	Introduce home leaders to congregation, annonce forthcoming home meetings.	Oct. 13: Worship Service.	To keep people informed of the continuing plan, and that home meetings will soon begin, to which each one will be invited.	More congregational "ownership" of the assessment, and persons alerted to soon being invited to a home meeting.

WHO	DOES WHAT	WHEN	WHY ARE WE DOING THIS?	EXPECTED RESULTS
Home Leaders	Personally invite all persons assigned to them, getting indication whether the date will fit their schedule.	Oct. 13-27	Each person must be personally invited by their leader, allowed to ask questions, indicate interest and whether date is satisfactory.	Every person personally invited to a home meeting. A list of those who cannot attend due to schedule conflicts.
Steering Committee and Home Leaders	Exchange names of persons who cannot attend home meetings to which invited due to schedule conflicts. Review home meeting design.	Oct. 28: Evening Meeting	To reassign persons who cannot attend home meeting to which first invited. Refresh memory regarding home meeting design.	Reassigning completed. Leaders ready to conduct home meetings.
Home Leaders	Invite new persons assigned to them.	Oct. 27–Nov. 2	To be sure no person need miss a home meeting due to schedule conflict.	A greater percentage of persons attending the home meeting.
Home Leaders	Conduct home meetings.	Nov. 2–Dec. 15	Home meetings will allow the people to become vitally involved in assessing their church by allowing each one to express his/her opinions, hear from a number of other members and to discuss personal hopes/dreams regarding the future of "our church."	A large amount of information regarding the major problems and opportunities of "our church," which can be used to set new directions and goals.

WHO	DOES WHAT	WHEN	WHY ARE WE DOING THIS?	EXPECTED RESULTS
Statistical Information Team	Gather all important statistical and demographic information about the church and community. Prepare this information for presentation in such a way that it will be helpful and interesting to the congregation.	Oct. 13–Jan. 15	This type of information will not be gathered in the home meetings.	Information to help the congregation understand its present condition and future possibilities.
Steering Committee, Home Leaders & Statistical Information Team	Compile the data, prepare narrative summaries and assessment report.	Jan. 1-10	To put the material into a suitable form for reporting to congregation and program units.	1. Categories of information. 2. Summary of each category. 3. Narrative assessment report.
Steering Committee	Report assessment findings to administrative board.	Jan. 15: Special Board Meeting	To inform board of the results and make suggestions for possible use of the material.	The Board prepared to present material to congregation and decide further uses of the material.
Administrative Board & Steering Committee	Worship service to celebrate the work, participation and results of the assessment process. To publicly thank the workers.	Jan. 25: Worship Service	To connect the worship life of the church with the work of the assessment project.	A celebrative service for a significant event in the life of "our church."
Administrative Board & Steering Committee	Make assessment report to the congregation.	Feb. 3	It is essential that the congregation know the results of the assessment and have a chance to talk about it.	An informed congregation with new commitment to change and programs called for by the assessment.

Index